ALASKA GEOGRAPHIC.

ALASKA WHALES and Whaling
Volume 5, Number 4, 1978

⚓ Narwhals

⚓ Grays

⚓ Bowhead and Belugas

⚓ Blue

Sperm ⚓

⚓ Humpbacks

Fin ⚓

⚓ Minke

♂ SEI

♂ KILLERS

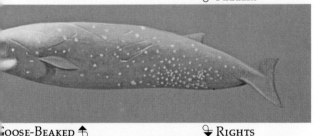

♂ GOOSE-BEAKED   ♀ RIGHTS

The Alaska Geographic Society

To teach many more to better know and use our natural resources

About This Issue: Perhaps more than any other issue, ALASKA WHALES AND WHALING has been a compilation of efforts on several fronts. Dr. Victor Scheffer, long a world-renowned zoologist, set the tone for this issue with his introduction to the great whales and their three-dimensional world. Dr. John Bockstoce, an expert on whaling in Alaska, provided a foundation around which to describe various facets of commercial and subsistence whaling. Lael Morgan, Associate Editor of *ALASKA*® magazine, provided information on specific aspects of modern cetacean research—whale sounds, whale watching and whales in captivity—and outlined the history of the whaling stations which dotted the Alaskan coast in past years. Charles Jurasz, a high school science teacher in Juneau, and his wife Virginia have told what it's like to cruise among the humpbacks of Southeastern doing field research on the great whales.

Stephen Leatherwood, Naval Ocean Systems Center; Randall R. Reeves, Smithsonian Institution; and Dr. George Harry, Dr. Howard Braham, Dale W. Rice, Clifford H. Fiscus, Allen A. Wolman and Roger W. Mercer, all of the Marine Mammal Division, National Marine Fisheries Service in Seattle, helped immeasurably with the profiles of the fifteen major whale species which inhabit Alaskan waters.

Taking photos of whales is difficult at best and we thank the many contributors who shared their photos of these gentle yet gigantic creatures. Special mention is given to James Hudnall and Gary Carter for their underwater shots of humpbacks, to Dr. Robbins Barstow and Donald Sineti of the Connecticut Cetacean Society for information and drawings of the whale species, and to Richard Ellis for his skillful paintings of the great whales.

We thank Dr. Erna Gunther, former professor of anthropology and an expert on Northwest Coast Indians, and Dr. Raymond M. Gilmore, of the Natural History Museum, San Diego, for reviewing portions of the manuscript. And we are grateful to Dr. Lydia Black for the research opportunity provided by her translation of early Aleut manuscripts in *Arctic Anthropology*.

Editors: Robert A. Henning, Marty Loken, Barbara Olds, Lael Morgan.
Associate Editor: Penny Rennick
Editorial Assistance: Jim Rearden, Robert N. De Armond, Tim Jones, Betty Johannsen
Designer: Roselyn Pape
Cartographer: Jon Hersh

THE ALASKA GEOGRAPHIC SOCIETY is a nonprofit organization exploring new frontiers of knowledge across the lands of the polar rim, learning how other men and other countries live in their Norths, putting the geography book back in the classroom, exploring new methods of teaching and learning—sharing in the excitement of discovery in man's wonderful new world north of 51°16'.

MEMBERS OF THE SOCIETY RECEIVE *Alaska Geographic*®, a quality magazine in color which devotes each quarterly issue to monographic in-depth coverage of a northern geographic region or resource-oriented subject.

MEMBERSHIP DUES in The Alaska Geographic Society are $20 for initiation and the first year, $16 thereafter. (Eighty percent of the first year's dues is for a one-year subscription to *Alaska Geographic*® magazine.) Order from The Alaska Geographic Society, Box 4-EEE, Anchorage, Alaska 99509; (907) 243-1484.

MATERIAL SOUGHT: The editors of *Alaska Geographic*® seek a wide variety of informative material on the lands north of 51°16' on geographic subjects—anything to do with resources and their uses (with heavy emphasis on quality color photography)—from Alaska, Northern Canada, Siberia, Japan—all geographic areas that have a relationship to Alaska in a physical or economic sense. (In the fall of 1978 editors were seeking photographs and other materials on the following subjects: Stikine River drainage; shellfish and shellfisheries of Alaska; Aleutian Islands; Yukon River and its tributaries; Wrangell and Saint Elias Mountains; and Alaska's Great Interior.) We do not want material done in excessive scientific terminology. A query to the editors is suggested. Payments are made for all material upon publication.

CHANGE OF ADDRESS: The post office does not automatically forward *Alaska Geographic*® when you move. To insure continuous service, notify us six weeks before moving. Send us your new address and zip code (and moving date), your old address and zip code, and if possible send a mailing label from a copy of *Alaska Geographic*®. Send this information to *Alaska Geographic*® Mailing Offices, 130 Second Avenue South, Edmonds, Washington 98020.

Second-class postage paid at Edmonds, Washington 98020.

Printed in U.S.A.

Registered Trademark: *Alaska Geographic*. Library of Congress catalog card number 72-92087.
ISSN 0361-1353; key title *Alaska Geographic*.
ISBN 0-88240-114-9

Paintings by RICHARD ELLIS

INTRODUCTION

By Dr. Victor B. Scheffer

Alaska's Whales

If you were to cruise in a low-flying plane from the arctic coast of Alaska southward to the Aleutian Islands, you might, in a single day, see 10 species of great whales. Nowhere else in the United States could you do so, for only Alaska has marine waters sufficiently vast, rich and diverse to support that many kinds. I must add that you would have to be *very* lucky to see all 10 in one day, for the populations of some species are extremely low. Roughly in the order of their worldwide abundance today, the Alaskan great whales are the sperm, gray, minke, fin, sei, blue, humpback, bowhead and right. (Other smaller whales found in Alaskan waters include the killer, beluga, goose-beaked, Bering Sea beaked, giant bottlenose and narwhal.)

My sharpest memory of whales anywhere and anytime is fixed on a moment 30 years ago in Alaska's Icy Strait. With my legs braced on the deck of a rolling ship and my face buried in the hood of an old-fashioned Graflex, I was trying to photograph the vapor spouts of a pod of humpbacks. By leading them—anticipating where they would rise—I was getting the shots I wanted. Suddenly the camera's view plate filled with an impossible sight—a dark body, dripping with jewels, rising from the sea and into the sky. Astonished, I raised my head for a better look, failed to press the trigger, and failed to capture an image that few have seen—the breaching of a 40-ton whale.

Much of what is known about the secret lives of whales has, in fact, been learned through chance encounters of this kind. Now and then a mariner will

A prominent dorsal fin and crisp black-and-white markings are keys to the identification of a killer whale. (K. C. Balcomb)

A humpback cow (below) and calf. Baby humpbacks need practice in diving, breathing and breaching and frequently seem to play around their mothers while the larger animals rest. (James Hudnall)

glimpse a pair of whales mating (belly-to-belly) or a female giving birth, or he will, as I once did, surprise a pod of killer whales attacking a larger species. Corpses found entangled in submarine cables have mutely revealed that a humpback may dive to at least 390 feet (off Sitka), a killer whale to 3,378 feet (off Vancouver Island), and a sperm to 3,720 feet (off Peru).

My fleeting glimpse of the breaching humpback was not my first close view of a whale, for in 1937 I had looked a humpback straight in the eye—on the platform of the old Akutan whaling station. But it was not the same. Here was simply a mountain of dark meat stripped of all symmetry and grace, steaming faintly in the chilly air.

When the first daring photographer dived in the path of a whale his eyes were opened to the far limits of power and beauty that life can reach. He rose to the surface, shaken. When television first brought whales into our homes we first began to see them as living creatures. No longer were they simply "marine rawstuffs"—inert, cheap sources of pet foods, mink foods, fertilizers and oils.

Why Do Whales Matter?

The great whale has become symbolic of today's campaign to preserve nature. Not only is it the greatest creature the world has ever known, but the mystery of its life recalls the deep and unexplored regions of human life, while its torn and wasted populations reveal what men can do to a vital resource.

Our fascination with whales is compounded by their mystery, their wildness and their behavior traits resembling those of humans. Many whales live in families, play in the moonlight, talk to one another

and care for one another in distress. We are drawn to them because we sense that the bloodlines of the whale and the human long ago were one. Some of us, moreover, credit whales not only with feelings but with rational thoughts.

But I am little moved by the argument that whales are intelligent as we are intelligent, and for that reason deserve our respect. I admit that the sperm whale has a brain of 20 pounds, as against mine of only 3, but I'm not sure that admitting whales to our club would be the best way of demonstrating our respect. We smart humans seem to spend a dreadful amount of effort inventing ways to knock each other off and to foul our habitat—when we're not planning to leave it behind altogether for new homes among the stars. Would it not be better to turn the argument around—to say that whales should be respected because they're *different*?

Zoologists (I among them) are attracted to whales because they so clearly prove their animal right to exist. Although every kind of animal on earth today is a specialist and is, by the very fact of its survival, "successful," whales are remarkably so. We admire them as we admire the more accomplished of our own fellows. At some unknown time between 60 and 100 million years ago, the land ancestors of whales faced the challenge of a chilling, fluid, three-dimensional and salty ocean. Ignoring (so to speak) their handicaps as warm-blooded, air-breathing, milk-giving, four-legged beasts, they plunged into the ocean and conquered it. Every modern whale is the end point and the splendid climax of a struggle to survive.

The finer details of whale evolution are still hidden. No missing links matching the idealized, land-dwelling protowhale have yet been found in the

Prince William Sound is a major summer feeding area for humpback whales. This animal thrust its bulk above the surface near Chenega Island, 36 miles southeast of Whittier in the western part of the sound. (John Hall)

7

The lack of a dorsal fin, a mottled gray color and barnacles on its head identify this as a gray whale, a species which is thought to be intermediate between the balaenopterid, or grooved, whales and the balaenid, or smooth, whales. (Stephen Leatherwood, NOSC)

fossil record. No good explanation has been offered for the splitting of ancestral stocks into the modern 10 species of great whales. Zoologists understand rather clearly how the evolution of *land* mammals (more than 4,000 species) must have been shaped by natural barriers such as mountains, deserts and rivers, which kept the drifting bloodlines apart and steadily widened the differences among them. But the world ocean is largely one ocean, having only the barriers of continents, sea-ice fields and water temperature zones. For lack of a better hypothesis, zoologists suppose that these barriers did in fact serve as wedges to split the few ancestral whales into many.

The beginning whale was in the ocean, then of the ocean. It was apart from the waters and then a part of the waters—the two inseparable. The moaning of the whale is a stirring of profound thoughts.

Whales Practice Multiple Use

The modern whales and their smaller relatives in the order of Cetacea are amazingly diverse. The harbor porpoise, smallest of the oceanic lot, weighs from 100 to 200 pounds, while the blue whale weighs up to 200 *tons* (or did before the whalemen came). The Chinese lake dolphin is totally blind from birth; some of the beaked whales have only two functional teeth; the bowhead calf at birth must adjust quickly from a blood-heat chamber to an ice-filled sea; the gray whale may travel 10,000 round-trip miles a year between its feeding and its breeding grounds.

The great whales are able to coexist, even to sharing some of the same oceanic pastures, because they long ago hit upon the principle of multiple use, a principle which modern land-use planners are still struggling to apply. Each whale has its own preferred diet of plankton, fish, squid or mammal—or

combinations thereof. Although these diets overlap, each kind of whale plays its own role. It fills its own ecologic niche.

Alaska's Special Link to Whales

The circumpolar waters of the Northern Hemisphere, including Alaska, have served as a special testing ground for whales. Three unique species—the bowhead, white (beluga) and narwhal—live here and nowhere else in the world. They have no counterparts in the Southern Hemisphere.

If Alaska needs a state mammal, the bowhead will do nicely. It is a pioneer; it has learned to find the best and to endure the worst in its demanding environment.

In the centuries ahead, Alaska is, I think, destined to become more than a place from which to extract oil, minerals and virgin trees, and a place to watch the erosion of the ancient soil which lies beneath those trees. Because of its hugeness, its 33,904 miles of tidal shoreline, and its wealth of natural habitats, it will surely become America's host state. I don't mean simply a vacation land (that tired phrase of the travel agent) but a land where a proud people will preserve and display to world visitors an enormous laboratory of creation. Like Washington, D.C., Alaska increasingly will be viewed as a national and international shrine. Men and women will visit it with the same sort of interest in its whales that they now have in its famous sea bird colonies, its fur seal rookeries and its caribou herds.

Alaska without whales would not be Alaska. I think of a vapor plume standing suddenly against the green walls of Lynn Canal, followed moments later by *CHUF-F-F*! I think of the roily wakes of feeding minke whales punctuating the surface of Unalaska Bay; and the distant turmoil—attended by swooping gulls—of a gray whale beset by killer whales; and the lifting of a 12-foot flipper at dawn like a serpent dimly seen; and the strange ellipses printed into sea ice by the warm backs of resting white whales. All these are Alaska.

The sheltered waters of Alaska will increasingly be used for research on whales (and I mean *humane* research). You will read in this issue about John Vania's experiment in repelling white whales with underwater sound, thereby controlling their predation upon salmon. And you will read of the Jurasz family's discovery of the "bubblenet" feeding of the humpback whale, first recorded in quiet waters near Auke Bay.

The Whale Imperiled

But to think only of Alaska's great whales is to ignore the larger populations of the North Pacific of which the Alaskan stocks (except for the bowhead) are a seasonal or a marginal part. Whales recognize no national boundaries. To preserve them will call for a kind of international cooperation more complex and more sensitive than any recorded in the history of wildlife management.

As I review the past and envision the future of the world's great whales, I see little reason for optimism. They are in peril. Having overhunted most of the species, we continue to pursue the rest. Whales are suddenly opposed by a new enemy—one which millions of years of evolutionary training have ill

During an early May 1977 flight over the Beaufort Sea, 17 miles east of Point Barrow, Bruce Krogman, a National Marine Fisheries Service wildlife biologist, took this photograph of six bowhead whales "engaged in reproductive activity." Clearly visible at the right is a male bowhead that has rolled on its side to clasp a female with its flippers (note penis almost midway between the male's flipper and fluke). The female is in a belly-up posture, apparently to avoid her suitors. The four other bowheads, Krogman said, continued to "mill around" the male and female during the 15-minute observation period. Krogman and other NMFS Marine Mammal Division biologists are studying bowhead whales in the Arctic for the Outer Continental Shelf Environmental Assessment Program, NOAA, funded by the Bureau of Land Management. Scientists believe that the spectacular creatures—up to 60 feet in length and weighing perhaps a ton per foot—mate during the spring as they migrate north from the Bering Sea to the Chukchi and Beaufort seas. (Reprinted from *ALASKA*® magazine)

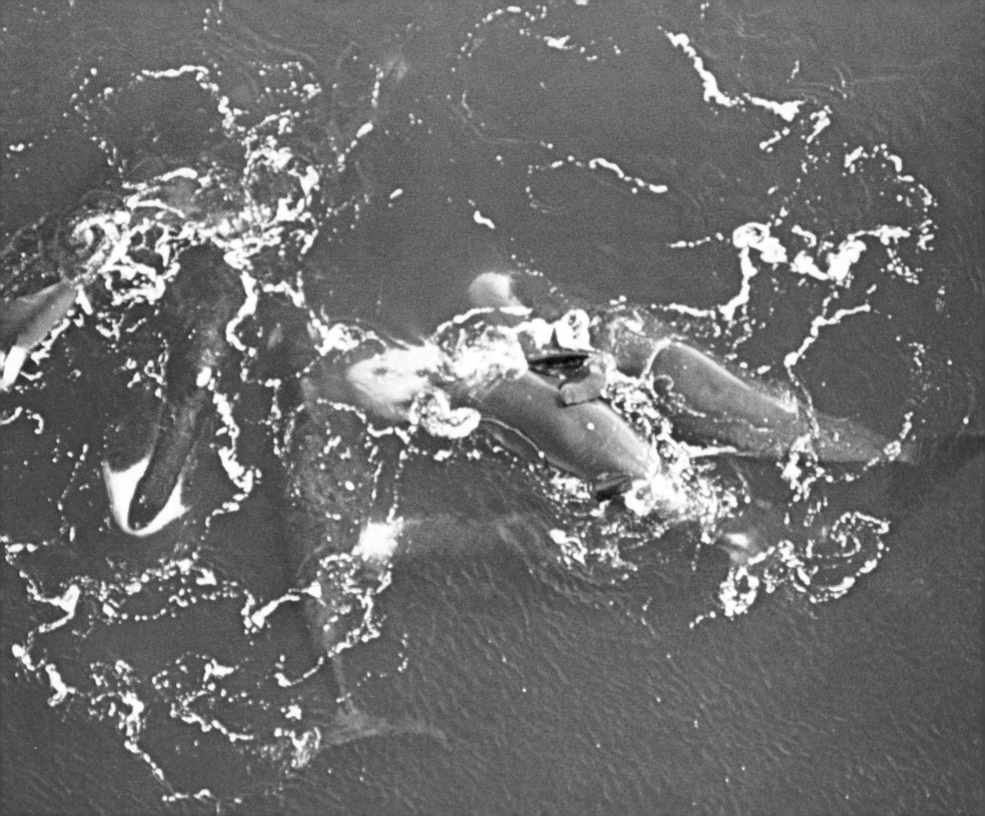

LEFT — The 10-foot fluke of a gray whale is momentarily suspended as the animal dives. (William Rossiter) BELOW — Baleen from a gray whale. (Therese L. Hoban)

prepared them to meet. In the Southern Ocean where the whale hunters first ran wild, the biomass of whales is down to 18% of its original size. Worldwide, the humpback whales are down to 7% of their prewhaling numbers; the blues to 6%, and the bowheads to a pitiful 3% to 6%. The original Asian-breeding stock of gray whales was wiped out in the 1930's.

The Monitor Consortium, headquartered in Washington, D.C., pointed out in 1978 that "there are now more countries whaling outside the International Whaling Commission than within that body. More than 3,500 whales, mostly from highly endangered species or populations, are killed without any regulation by whalers operating under the flags of Peru, Cyprus, Spain, Portugal, South Korea, North Korea, and, reportedly, the People's Republic of China and Taiwan. Most of these outlaw whalers are owned or supported by Japanese whaling companies. . . ."

So I'm convinced that several of the great whales

Close-up of the back of a gray whale. When swimming just below the surface, gray whales live up to their name because they appear to be uniformly gray. But in reality, the gray is mottled with splotches of lighter gray. (Cliff Hyatt)

are headed for extinction unless the world's leading nations press ever more firmly for a temporary ban on killing and for economic sanctions against outlaw whaling nations. It does not seem enough that the International Whaling Commission, in the five-year period ending in 1978, cut kill quotas to one-half. It does not seem enough that President Carter, in 1977, reaffirmed the continued support of the United States government for a 10-year worldwide moratorium on commercial whaling (which is a hope) and prohibition of commercial whaling within our 200-mile fishery zone (which is a fact).

It is because zoologists know so little about the reasons behind wildlife population changes that they worry about the future of whales. Witness the histories of two stocks which were reduced to a few hundred individuals in the early years of the present century. The gray whales of the North Pacific were given protection from hunting in the 1930's and immediately began to increase; they now number between 10,000 and 15,000. The right whales of the

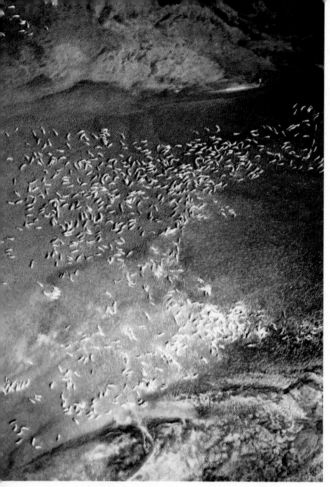

Hundreds of belugas were calving at Somerset Island in the Canadian Arctic on July 30, 1973. The greatest concentration of animals was near the mouth of a river which drains into Cunningham Inlet, where the temperature is 10 degrees warmer than in darker inlet waters at left. Most of the belugas were in about 50 feet of water . . . the majority of adults and newborn calves were 10 to 30 feet below the surface. (Douglas Heyland, Quebec Department of Tourism, Game and Fish, courtesy of Arctic Environmental Information and Data Center. Reprinted from *ALASKA*® magazine)

Montague Strait at the southwest edge of Prince William Sound, with Knight Islar the background, is the scene for this spectacular photo of a breaching humpb (Neil and Betty Johann

North Pacific were given similar protection but did not recover; they still number only 200 to 300 individuals.

Why did the right whales fail to respond? At the point in time when they were nearly gone, did they have trouble finding mates? (I simplify here. Among large wild mammals, mating entails more than boy meets girl. Often it calls for the stimulus of a third party and always it calls for mutual timing in the sexual cycles of male and female.) Were the whales so fragmented that their "educational system" broke down, leaving young whales unsure of the traditional migration routes? Did other, more competitive, whales such as the seis and humpbacks preempt the food pastures once dominated by the right whales? No one knows, which is why most zoologists want a ban on whaling until they learn more about the ecology of the target species.

Moreover, zoologists fear that whales are suffering today not only from explosive harpoons but from hidden poisons. They are surely being exposed to insect sprays, weed-killers, tetraethyl lead from automobile exhausts and manufacturing wastes such as cadmium, mercury and arsenic. These contaminants in solution in rivers or in rain enter the ocean—nature's great sink—and are taken up by microscopic plants. Many of them appear intact in the tissues of sea mammals. Whatever harm they do by causing disease and by depressing reproductive success is rarely possible to measure, yet it should not be ignored.

Some zoologists believe that it is safe to continue whaling against two of the North Pacific stocks—those of the minke and the sperm—which are not yet clearly endangered. They argue, typically, that to harvest a renewable resource is

"rational." Well, so it is, but is it necessarily right? Growing numbers of Americans are saying, "We reserve the privilege of discriminating—of deciding what species we will kill (or let be killed) and what species we will spare. Although we are willing to kill rabbits, pigs and chickens, we are not willing to kill whales. Although our reasons are frankly emotional, we think that emotion is one of the better reasons for deciding to spare whales." These Americans are making a choice between values which cannot be compared, one expressed in scientific-technologic language, the other in wordless feelings.

As a wildlife management zoologist nearing the end of a 40-year career, I had long supposed that because killing whales is a cultural habit, and because dead whales can be sold for money, and because whalemen feel a common bond in the hunting of their prey, that killing is justified. Now I believe that to destroy the world's greatest living forms is among the greatest of wrongs that we can do to a species other than our own.

As the whale is great, so to cherish it can be proof of our greatness.

Meanwhile, and for a little longer, the great whale glides through the sea, feeling its vibrations and reading its meaning by senses it has gained through eons of time. Had the whale been created only to deepen our sense of wonder, that were enough, for it is imagination that makes us human. □

Editor's note: *Dr. Scheffer, a retired wildlife management zoologist (U.S. Fish & Wildlife Service) is the author of* Year of the Whale — *recommended to all who are fascinated by the great whales.*

The crew of the whaler *Rosario* in early spring, 1898. The *Rosario* became trapped in the ice west of Point Barrow in the fall of 1897, and eventually was crushed in July 1898. (Private collection)

Whalers butcher a whale at Akutan in the Aleutian Islands, circa 1930's.

By JOHN BOCKSTOCE

History of Commercial Whaling in Arctic Alaska

Although the Eskimos of Northwestern Alaska had developed a sophisticated whaling culture before A.D. 1000, it was not until 700 years later that stirrings in the Yankee whaling industry brought about changes that would draw these two peoples together in pursuit of the bowhead whale. In the 1750's New England whalemen began to carry tryworks (rendering pots) aboard their vessels, allowing them to render oil from blubber at sea and thus to cruise far beyond the waters to which they had been confined when they relied on shore stations for processing. Soon these ships began reaching deep into the South Atlantic; then in 1791 the first American whaleship rounded Cape Horn and found the rich sperm whaling grounds off the coast of Chile. But the whalemen pressed farther into the Pacific, reaching Hawaii before 1820, the coast of Japan grounds a few

years later, and most importantly, in 1835, the first whaleship cruised "on Kodiak," finding the abundant sperm and right whales in the Gulf of Alaska. Some ships quickly passed through the Aleutians and discovered right whales in Bristol Bay and off the coast of Kamchatka.

By 1847 the waters of the entire Pacific Ocean except the northern Bering Sea had been scouted by American vessels, and in the following year the most important discovery was made. In 1848 Captain Thomas Roys, restless and resourceful, sailed his bark, the *Superior* of Sag Harbor, Long Island, through northern mists into seas unknown to whalemen and with a frightened, nearly mutinous crew forced his way through Bering Strait into the Arctic Ocean.

Roys decided to go north because he had noted that Captain

INSET — Six-foot tall M. G. Bartlett stands between two bundles of baleen on the deck of the *Patterson*. Bartlett was a helper on the schooners *Nanuk* and *Patterson*. (C. T. Pedersen, reprinted from *A Whaler & Trader in the Arctic*)

18

The whaler *Elvira* was built in Misato, Japan, in 1898. The ship made two whaling voyages, the first in 1912 under Captain C. T. Pedersen. Later the *Elvira* became trapped in the ice near Barter Island on the arctic coast and was lost. (San Francisco Maritime Museum)

Frederick William Beechey had reported seeing large numbers of whales in 1826 and 1827 during his explorations in the waters later called the Chukchi Sea. Although whalemen were frequently intrepid, the dual dangers of rudimentary charts and icy seas terrified Roys's crew (justifiably, as it turned out: more than 100 whaleships would be lost there in the next 60 years) and he was forced to cajole and threaten them once they passed the central Bering Sea. But his determination paid off; when the fog lifted in Bering Strait one day in July, they began to take bowhead whales so quickly that in a month they had filled their ship and sailed for Hawaii with 1,800 barrels (1 barrel held 31½ gallons) of oil in the hold.

When Roys reached Honolulu he wrote Samuel Damon—the missionary who was the editor of Hawaii's newspaper, *The Friend*—telling him of the vast numbers of whales he had seen. Roys said that they were oil-rich, baleen-laden, slow-moving and docile, and that one whale he had seen was so large that he dared not take it. (He estimated it would have yielded 300 barrels; an average bowhead gave 100 barrels, and a gray whale, 25.) Damon published the report in *The Friend*, and whalemen quickly carried it round the world.

News of Roys's discovery touched off an oil rush to Bering Strait. In 1849 more than 70 ships sailed there, and the number continued to grow annually, spurred by reports of large catches, until in 1852 more than 200 vessels were operating in those waters. But the 1852 season was poor and 1853 and 1854 were disastrous. Assuming those waters to have been fished out, the fleet virtually deserted them in 1855, 1856 and 1857, turning its attention to the bowheads and right whales of the Okhotsk Sea. But the catches made there quickly declined, and in 1858 the ships began to return to Bering Strait.

From then until the industry collapsed half a century later, the majority of the North Pacific fleet went annually to Bering Strait, its most productive waters, and quickly established a pattern of cruising that would vary only slightly in the succeeding years. Leaving the ports of New England in the autumn, the ships would round Cape Horn in the southern summer and then cruise in the temperate waters of the Pacific, usually for sperm or gray whales, until March, when most of the fleet would stop in Hawaii to take on fresh provisions and to recruit a few new men for their northern summer. After a few weeks in Hawaii,

they would leave for the north and after a month's sail reach the melting pack ice in the central Bering Sea. From then on the men maintained a constant watch for bowheads as the ships worked their way through the leads along the Siberian shore from Cape Navarin to Saint Lawrence Island. Once they had reached Bering Strait, usually in mid-June, the ice would block them from entering the Arctic Ocean, and the bowheads would long since have passed through on their summer migration to their feeding grounds in the Beaufort Sea. To pass the time until late July when the ice would open and allow the ships to reach Point Barrow to meet the whales again, the whalemen traded with the Natives for furs and ivory or, in the 1860's and 1870's—when oil prices were still relatively high—took walruses in vast numbers.

When the ice had receded far enough to let the ships pass along the Alaska shore beyond Icy Cape, they began to intersect the whales on their migration from the Beaufort Sea to their autumn feeding grounds near Herald Island in the Chukchi Sea. By late August most of the fleet had followed the bowheads to the west, where the whalemen frequently made their best catches. But although these waters could be lucrative, they could also be treacherous, for in late September the ice would begin to creep south with two great arms girdling the Chukchi Sea,

Proud whalers line up beside a right whale taken off Kodiak Island. The animal measured 15 feet high, 22 feet wide, 65 feet long and weighed approximately 250 tons. (San Francisco Maritime Museum)

The whaling schooner *Olga* was wrecked at Nome, Alaska, in October 1909. (San Francisco Maritime Museum, reprinted from *The ALASKA SPORTSMAN*®)

reaching south along the Alaska and Siberian shores and surrounding the relatively open area near Herald Island. Nevertheless, the whalemen were aware of this danger and often calculated to the last possible day when it would be safe to run for Bering Strait, slipping through between the two converging bodies of ice.

However, the industry's star quickly ceased its ascent: 1865 marked the beginning of a series of tragedies that plagued the fleet for the next 40 years. In 1865 the last encounter of the Civil War took place near Bering Strait when the Confederate raider *Shenandoah* burned 20 whaleships and caused the wreck of another; in 1871 32 ships were abandoned between Point Belcher and Icy Cape when the ice trapped them on a lee shore; in 1876 12 more ships were lost near Point Barrow; and in almost every other year one or two vessels were wrecked or crushed in the ice.

With these terrible losses in ships and men came a slow decline in the price of whale oil, the result of the petroleum industry progressively undercutting the whale oil market. To offset this decline the whalemen sought to increase their catches. The bowheads already had been harvested to such a level that the whalemen had difficulty in finding them during the "spring season" and the "middle season" before they began the "fall season" in the waters between Point Barrow and Herald Island. Consequently, they turned to the vast herds of walruses exclusively, using skiffs to quietly approach the sleeping pods before opening fire with large-caliber rifles, they would chop out the ivory, then strip the carcass of blubber and float it back to the ship for rendering. An average-sized walrus yielded about 20 gallons of oil and the slaughter was enormous. Between 1868, when the hunt began in earnest, and 1880, when it was largely abandoned, 100,000 walruses may have been taken.

Despite the walrus hunting, by 1875 the industry was ill indeed. The price of animal oils continued to fall, and the market showed little prospect of reviving. But what temporarily saved the industry and gave it 30 years of life was the baleen, or whalebone, market. In the late 1870's the fashion industry began to require greater and greater amounts of baleen, the plates that hang from a bowhead's upper jaw and are used to filter plankton from the water. This flexible and resilient material, used for corset stays and skirt hoops, was the only commodity available in the 19th century that approximated the qualities of modern plastics.

As the price of baleen began to rise, enterprising whaling merchants in New Bedford and San Francisco saw the advantages of using steam auxiliary whaling ships to pursue the increasingly elusive bowheads among the ice floes where no sail-powered vessel could go without great risk. The steamers were an immediate success and were widely copied in the 1880's, while the price of baleen rose ever higher and the number of bowheads declined further.

It was these two factors, the rise of baleen's price and the depletion of the bowheads, that stimulated the creation of commercial shore whaling stations and ultimately brought the Eskimos of Northwestern Alaska into close contact with white men. Since before A.D. 1000 the Eskimos had been whaling effectively at the spring leads in the ice, skillfully taking whales as they moved north to their summer feeding grounds. Their equipment was perfectly suited to the conditions: sealskin-covered *umiaks* of great resiliency and inflated sealskin drag-floats attached to the harpoon line to retard and tire the whale in its flight.

In 1884 the Pacific Steam Whaling Company of San Francisco, acting on the advice of Edward Perry "Ned" Herendeen, decided to establish a shore whaling station at Point Barrow using the abandoned U.S. Army Signal Corps expedition's quarters. Herendeen had been the expedition's interpreter from 1881 to 1883 and had closely observed the Eskimo shore whaling methods. When he returned to San Francisco, he convinced Josiah Knowles, the company's manager, that those whales, unreachable with ships, could be profitably taken in the Eskimo fashion.

Although Eskimo and Yankee whaling technology had evolved independently, the implements were surprisingly

ABOVE — Clad in one-piece waterproof suits, two butchers crawl into a hole cut in the whale's stomach where they carve meat and throw it to the women on the shore ice. (Lusk Collection, Archives, University of Alaska, Fairbanks)
LEFT — Flensing blubber from a whale. (Barrett Willoughby Collection, Archives, University of Alaska, Fairbanks)

21

similar. The principal difference, apart from bomb-lance shoulder guns and darting guns, was in the Eskimos' use of the drag-float, thus avoiding the Yankees' "Nantucket sleigh-ride" in which the boat itself was towed by the whale—with potentially disastrous consequences in icy seas.

Herendeen returned to Point Barrow in 1884 to establish the station. Although the 1885 season was unproductive, the men took several whales the following spring, and the success of the venture was assured. When the news of this new technique reached San Francisco in the autumn of 1886, it prompted the S.H. Frank Company to attempt a similar operation at Northern Alaska's other great whaling site, Point Hope. Thus began projects that would continue vigorously until 1910 and would alter the complexion of the arctic coast.

Because the price of baleen continued high, the stations were immediately profitable and within a few years 15 were established between Point Barrow and Cape Thompson. The stations usually operated with a skeleton staff and counted on putting out several crews—occasionally as many as 20—manned largely by Eskimos. Because eight men were needed for each crew, the competition for manpower was intense, with each station offering its men a retainer fee consisting of as much as a year's supply of flour, as well as rifles, cartridges and other food and manufactured goods in payment for the two-month whaling season.

The stations' presence converted the Eskimos into commercial whalemen, and had two principal effects on the Natives. First, the population of Northwestern Alaska was concentrated around the stations, primarily at Point Barrow and Point Hope, drawing many inland Natives from the Brooks Range and from the Kobuk-Noatak drainage and depopulating some areas. Second, the stipends paid to Eskimos created wants and needs for manufactured goods that could only be satisfied through whaling, or later, after the industry had collapsed, by the fur trade. The fur trade economy led to the dispersal of the population once again. Some Eskimos operated their own crews alongside the stations' boats and quickly became wealthy themselves, competing effectively with the companies.

Through the 1880's the whalemen found it more and more difficult to catch bowheads, and in response they began to press eastward past Point Barrow, along the coast of northern Alaska,

Hartson Bodfish in full arctic dress holds a 44-pound mammoth tusk on the deck of the *Beluga*. Bodfish was first mate on the *Mary D. Hume* when she steamed east to Cape Bathurst in the Canadian Arctic and, in July 1891, came upon the summer feeding grounds of the bowhead. This was the last major whaling ground to be discovered by the American whaling industry. (Old Dartmouth Historical Society Whaling Museum)

an unknown region to the whalers, who had shunned it for fear of being caught between the hammer and anvil of the icepack and the shore. In a few years the ships had probed beyond the Colville River Delta, and in 1888 arrived at Barter Island, the first foreign vessels in those waters since the searches for Sir John Franklin more than 30 years before.

Strangely enough, it was not the whaling fleet but an itinerant whaleman who discovered the bowheads' summer feeding grounds. In 1887 Charles Brower, the manager of the Cape Smythe Whaling and Trading Company at Point Barrow, heard from Eskimo traders returning from the Mackenzie River Delta that they had seen large number of whales in its shallow waters. With the same energy and enterprise that he displayed throughout his long life, Brower outfitted one of his men, Joe Tuckfield, with a whaleboat, an Eskimo crew and provisions and sent them east in 1888 on a reconnaissance voyage. Tuckfield wintered in the delta, found game and driftwood abundant, had good relations with the Natives, and—most important—found the bowheads plentiful. He took one and brought the baleen with him when he returned to Point Barrow in 1889.

His report that whales were "as thick as bees" in Mackenzie Bay set off a baleen rush that ushered in the arctic whaling industry's last hurrah and pushed the whales—already severely reduced—toward extinction.

Before he reached Point Barrow, though, Tuckfield met a fleet of seven whaling steamers off the Colville Delta and gave them his news. The ships immediately set off for the east, passed Barter Island, and entered waters where whaleships had never ventured. They reached Herschel Island and sounded Pauline Cove, the harbor that soon became the hub of the industry's operations.

Having taken a few bowheads, the fleet retreated westward with the knowledge that wintering safely in the Western Arctic was possible and that it would save most of the short summer season for whaling rather than wasting it on the long unproductive voyage from the Pacific.

In 1890, the Pacific Steam Whaling Company sent its two smallest steamers, the *Mary D. Hume* (still afloat today in Seattle) and the *Grampus*, north to experiment in wintering and whaling from the advance base at Herschel Island. They were joined there by the little schooner *Nicoline*; and the three became the first whaleships to winter east of Point Barrow. Although the *Nicoline*, short of provisions, left for San Francisco as soon as the ice would allow in 1891 and the

The whaling bark *Mermaid* at anchor at Dutch Harbor in the Aleutians in 1900.
(San Francisco Maritime Museum)

A photographic display of activities of the Pacific Whaling Company dresses the windows of an elegant store. The sign invites visitors to come see the 60-ton, 55-foot whale at the Sante Fe Stone Depot. (San Francisco Maritime Museum)
INSET — Whaling gear. The darting gun, leaning diagonally, is shown only in part; the wooden handle is almost 6 feet long. The gun has a bomb and harpoon attached; the bomb is released when the trigger hits the whale. The trigger is the metal rod below the bomb. Also shown are a shoulder gun, bombs for the shoulder gun, and hand lances for spearing a wounded whale. (Photography Collection, Suzallo Library, University of Washington, reprinted from *A Whaler & Trader in the Arctic*)

24

Grampus went out soon after, the *Mary D. Hume* remained for another winter and found her "El Dorado," as her first mate, Hartson Bodfish, put it. The *Hume* went east to Cape Bathurst—where the muddy waters of the Mackenzie become clearer, having deposited enough silt to allow sunlight to penetrate and trigger a rich plankton bloom. There they found the bowheads' summer feeding grounds—their last refuge, and the last important whaling ground to be discovered by the American whaling industry.

When the *Hume* reached San Francisco in October 1892, she had made one of the most productive voyages in the history of American whaling, and her success touched off a frenzy of activity that would lead to more than 100 wintering voyages east of Point Barrow in the next 20 years.

The whaling fleet quickly moved into these distant waters and was immediately rewarded, but they so thoroughly suppressed the remainder of the bowhead population that the 1897 season was only moderately successful and subsequent seasons were rarely good. In retrospect it appears that the 1897 season signaled the beginning of the end for the industry, for in that disastrous year four ships were lost to the icepack and four others were forced to seek refuge in emergency quarters on the coast. Three of the lost ships were steamers; they were never replaced, and the Pacific Steam Whaling Company, always the industry's leader in foresight, began to wind down its arctic operations. (See "The Arctic Whaling Disaster of 1897" on page 27.)

Ironically, it was the very scarcity of the whales that saved them. As fewer and fewer were caught, the price of baleen rose higher, reaching more than $7 per pound at one point. But the high price invited cheaper substitutes and spring steel was soon introduced for corset stays. In one year, 1907, the price of baleen dropped nearly 75%, with the remaining market very soft indeed. From 1908 onward the few ships that cleared port as whalers were primarily fitted for fur trading voyages.

The whaling industry left an indelible mark on Northern Alaska. Many places will forever be associated with the industry and with the ships that were lost there—Point Barrow, Point Franklin, Icy Cape, and Point Hope—and the names of whalemen are perpetuated by their descendants in coastal Alaska who, like their ancestors, are whalers: Brower, Hopson,

Casks for water are towed ashore from a whaler near Port Clarence on the Seward Peninsula. The whalers, which followed the bowheads north in May and June generally could not work their way through the ice leads into the Arctic Ocean until late June. Consequently they put in at Port Clarence to take on water, make repairs, and get mail, supplies and coal from their tenders. (San Francisco Maritime Museum)

Gordon, Bodfish, Vincent, Tuckfield, Koenig and many others. And while the whaling industry brought about the first commercial development of Northern Alaska, it also indirectly touched off the second, for Charles Brower discovered the oil seeps in the Sagavanirktok Delta near Prudhoe Bay. ☐

Editor's note: *The author is Curator of Ethnology at the New Bedford, Massachusetts, Whaling Museum. His most recent book is* Steam Whaling in the Western Arctic, *a history of the last 30 years of the arctic whaling industry.*

The *Navarch* shortly after her launching in Bath, Maine.
(Bath Marine Museum, Bath, Maine)

By JOHN BOCKSTOCE

The Arctic Whaling Disaster of 1897

Editor's note: *This article has been excerpted from the journal of the National Archives,* Prologue, *Spring 1977, pages 27-42. It is reprinted here with permission of the author.*

Early in August 1897, the loss of the steam auxiliary whaling bark *Navarch* provided a gloomy harbinger of the events of September. The sturdy and powerful *Navarch*, built in Bath, Maine, only five years earlier, was the handsomest of the steam whalers. Her raking bow and clean, graceful lines belied the strength of her hull; she had been designed solely for the arctic fishery and consequently her hull had been reinforced to withstand the pressures of the ice floes she was to ram. In fact, the *Navarch* was typical of the design innovations incorporated in such steam auxiliaries. The first had been launched in 1879, part of the industry's response to the elusiveness and the declining number of bowhead whales. Instead of skirting the ice fields as sailing vessels did, the steamers, with their massive structural reinforcements and auxiliary power, were capable of forcing their way into the arctic fastnesses in pursuit of the increasingly valuable baleen found in the mouths of the bowheads. And when they had returned to San Francisco at the end of a cruise and their cargoes had been sold—to be made into corset stays and buggy whips—the profits more than compensated for the great expense of building them.

ABOVE — Charles Brower, who lived in the Arctic for more than 50 years, led 32 crew members of the *Navarch* away from the trapped vessel in hopes that a passing whaler would rescue them from the traveling ice floes. (Jarvis Collection, New Bedford Whaling Museum, courtesy of the author)

27

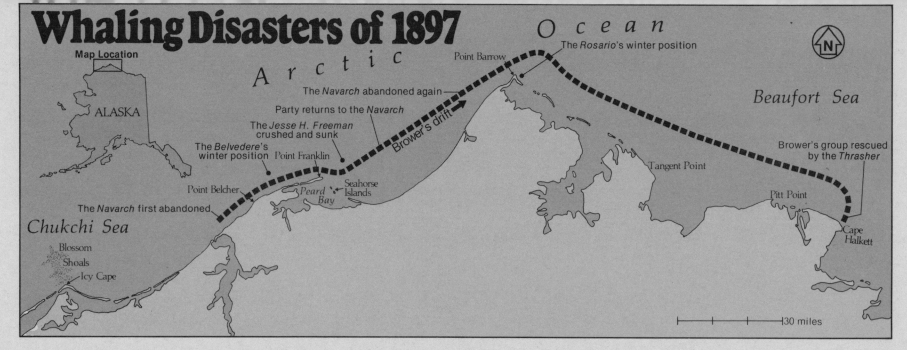

Whaling Disasters of 1897

Map Location

Arctic *Ocean*

ALASKA

Beaufort Sea

The *Rosario*'s winter position

Point Barrow

The *Navarch* abandoned again

Party returns to the *Navarch*

The *Jesse H. Freeman* crushed and sunk

The *Belvedere*'s winter position

Point Franklin

Brower's drift

Point Belcher

The *Navarch* first abandoned

Peard Bay

Seahorse Islands

Tangent Point

Brower's group rescued by the *Thrasher*

Pitt Point

Cape Halkett

Chukchi Sea

Blossom Shoals

Icy Cape

30 miles

In the spring of 1897, the whaling fleet from San Francisco, nineteen vessels, worked its way as usual through Bering Strait and into the Arctic as far as the melting ice floes permitted. This part of the arctic passage was generally regarded as routine. But when the fleet reached Icy Cape [see map], late in July, the crew's nonchalance, evident in the earlier part of the season, disappeared. Beyond Icy Cape the margin of the icepack is never far from shore, and the vessels, in order to reach the whales' summer feeding grounds east of Point Barrow in the Beaufort Sea, were forced to run the gauntlet between the shoal water along the coast and the menacing icepack at sea. . . .

Late in July or early in August the ice seldom retreats far from the coast of northwestern Alaska; the margin is usually not more than ten to twenty miles from Point Franklin and about twice that distance from Icy Cape. Later in the season, under continuous pressure from currents and southerly or easterly winds, it may move as many as one hundred miles from Point Barrow. In 1897, however, the ice was heavier than usual, the margin narrower. Late in July ten days of light northerlies had forced many small pieces of ice from the edge of the pack, driving them toward shore. The *Navarch*, the vanguard of the fleet, was moored to grounded ice about twenty miles beyond the Cape,[1] and there for more than a week the ice slowly packed around the

vessel. On the twenty-seventh she was boarded by Charles Brower, the manager of the H. Liebes Company whaling and trading station at Point Barrow. . . . Once aboard *Navarch* he viewed the encroaching ice with alarm. . . .

While the rest of the fleet lay in comparative safety near Icy Cape, the *Navarch*, with Brower aboard, was carried swiftly northeastward, ever farther from shore. By the third of August she had been carried about twenty-five miles northwest of Point Belcher.[2] Seeing that their situation was perilous, with little chance of escape for the ship, Capt. Joseph Whiteside decided to abandon her and attempt to reach the shore by crossing the moving ice floe with whaleboats. Brower, a veteran of shore whaling operations, was well acquainted with the rigors of hauling whaleboats over the broken and piled ice floes and was under no illusion about the difficulty of the task or about the fragility of the boats. He counseled Whiteside to add a four-inch false keel to the boats to protect their thin cedar planks from the ice and to carry canvas with him for quick repairs. Ignoring this advice, Whiteside added only an inch to the keels and did not carry any canvas.

The *Navarch* had to be abandoned on the third by all but eight of the crew, who decided to take their chances on remaining with the ship. The party, including Mrs. Whiteside, made slow progress, dragging their three boats to the southeast, opposite the direction they were drifting in. On the fourth they reached heavier ice, but the crew was soon exhausted and two of the boats, badly damaged, were abandoned. Later, on reaching the edge of the pack, the third boat was launched—against Brower's advice—in the dangerously swirling ice. It, too, was wrecked, and the party had no choice but to return to the ship, now a ten-mile trek back across the badly piled and broken ice.

The captain then broke down and, drinking heavily from a flask, declared that it was every man for himself. He ignored his wife, leaving Brower to assist her back to the ship.[3]

The group straggled up to the ship five days later,[4] but Brower knew there was no time to lose before starting out again. The other ships were unaware of the crew's predicament, and by then the *Navarch* had drifted nearly to Point Barrow. He realized that once past the point, the strong current that flowed along the coast forked, with one stream swinging west toward Wrangel Island a hundred miles north of Siberia and the other turning east into the Beaufort Sea. Thus their only real hope of safety lay in reaching land before they were swept past Point Barrow, "for beyond that no ship had ever drifted and returned except the (whaling bark) *Young Phoenix*, and she was frozen fast in the ice."[5]

He quickly set about building a light canvas boat along the lines of an Eskimo *umiak*. Brower's experience in hauling boats across the ice during spring whaling had shown him that whereas the whaleboat was difficult to transport and handle, the *umiak*—with its driftwood frame and sealskin covering—was light and tough. His boat, made with a hickory frame covered with oiled canvas, could hold ten men and was light enough to be carried by two.

The group started again on August 10. Brower agreed to go ahead, breaking trail for the others, and the captain with his wife were to follow with the boat. Late in the afternoon the vanguard reached the edge of the pack, only six miles from shore and a few miles south of the point. . . . As the men straggled up to Brower, he asked where the captain and the boat were. The last arrival told him that Captain Whiteside had ordered the boat, compass, food, and ammunition taken back to the ship. . . .

Brower knew that the only hope for the party of thirty-two men was to move into the current of ice flowing east around the point into the Beaufort Sea. To do so he knew that they must leave the solid older ice and reach the smaller drifting pieces of year-old ice, farther out at the pack's margin. Once in the Beaufort Sea, there was a chance, a small chance, that they would be sighted by a whaler. . . .

Eight days after leaving the ship, the party reached the edge of the pack ice somewhere east of Point Barrow. Although most of the men wanted to wait there, on relatively solid ice, in hope of being spotted, Brower urged them to join him on a small floe which might be blown to shore. He clinched his argument by pointing out that they might just as well die on a small piece of ice as on a large one.

Boarding an icecake twenty yards square, they drifted southeast for four days, until they were within two miles of Cape Halkett, about one hundred miles east of Point Barrow. Here on the twelfth day they saw the steam bark *Thrasher* coming toward them along the coast. A Siberian Eskimo at

The *Belvedere* offered temporary shelter to the crews of the *Freeman* and *Orca* after those ships were crushed in the ice. This photo was taken at the Seahorse Islands where the *Belvedere* could winter because the three crews made a path for her through the ice. (Reprinted from *A Whaler & Trader in the Arctic*) the *Thrasher's* masthead spotted something in the distance but thought it was a group of walrus on the ice. Knowing that they were rare east of Point Barrow, he called the figures to the attention of the officers on deck. They turned their glasses on the small party, and soon Brower and his men were rescued.[6] . . .

While the *Navarch* fell victim to the ice, the rest of the fleet, proceeding more cautiously, rounded Point Barrow without difficulty and reached the whaling ground near Herschel Island. The whaling season of 1897 was only moderately successful. By August 20 several whaling vessels that had reached Herschel Island earlier in the season or had wintered near there had begun to work their way west along the north coast of Alaska, following the bowheads as they migrated to their autumn feeding grounds in the western Chukchi Sea. On August 27, near Cape Halkett, the steam barks *Belvedere, Orca,* and *Jesse H. Freeman* found thickly scattered ice within a mile of the shore; by September 2 they had made only half the distance to Point Barrow and they found the ice hard on the land. But two days later they were able to move within ten miles of the point where they were joined by the steam bark *Alexander* and the schooner *Rosario,*[7] also returning west. . . .

A stiff westerly sprang up on the sixth of September as the ships reached Point Barrow, and by midnight the wind had reached gale force, bringing the ice down on the point and to within a half mile of shore elsewhere. During the next three days light winds allowed the icepack to ease off the shore slightly, and the ships were able to slip around to the west side of the point, but farther they could not go.[8]

But the dirty weather of the arctic autumn was upon them. On the tenth the wind shifted around to the north, lowering the temperature and causing ice to form on the patches of open water. Alive to the increasingly dangerous situation, Capt. Benjamin Tilton worked the *Alexander* close inshore on the west side of the point behind a long ridge of grounded ice, an unmelted remnant of a massive winter pressure ridge such as is often found parallel to shore there. Protected by it, Tilton quickly unloaded a year's supplies at Brower's whaling station, then left hurriedly, ramming ahead and breaking through the ridge as soon as the ice outside slackened off.[9] The *Alexander's* engineer described the fight to reach open water:

For eighteen hours it was "full speed astern," then "stop her" and then "full speed ahead," followed by the crash as we struck the icefield. Back and forth we went and every succeeding crash seemed to us down in the engine-room as though it would be our last. It did not seem possible that wood and iron could stand the strain much longer. After getting through the pack we had to fight our way through . . . miles of young ice an inch and a half thick. I can tell you when we reached [the] Sea Horse Island[s] and saw open water before us we were a happy set of men.[10]

The *Alexander* was the last vessel to leave the Arctic from Point Barrow that year. It is puzzling that as she was leaving, other ships did not attempt to break out with her. One observer wrote, "I suppose they think the ice will go off from the shore, and they can get out without bucking."[11] Nevertheless, the *Orca, Jesse H. Freeman, Belvedere,* and *Rosario* were anchored in a small area of open water southwest of the point, hemmed in on the east by the land, on the south by the pressure ridge, and on the north and west by the pack—and young ice was forming rapidly.[12] The captains were now fully aware of the danger of their situation. They faced every prospect of being forced to winter on an exposed coast where the ice would almost surely destroy their vessels—as it had destroyed others in 1871 and 1876—and none had the ten months' supplies aboard to feed their crews until breakup.

The *Rosario,* lacking auxiliary power, was forced to remain in the small patch of open water . . . west of Point Barrow. She could not escape, and was finally crushed the following July.[13] On the seventeenth, a week after the normally safe departure date, the other vessels began to fight their way out. The *Belvedere* and the *Orca,* more powerful than the *Jesse H. Freeman,* took the lead, ramming their way through the thickening ice. Brought to a standstill by heavy floes, they put their crews on the ice to blast with gunpowder while the ships rammed ahead. By the nineteenth they had made only six miles and lay off Brower's station. Their venture had cost them dearly. The *Orca* had lost her rudder, and the *Belvedere* had sprung hers badly. They were forced to spend a day there making repairs.[14] . . .

Despite the increasing danger and necessity of speed, Capt.

The *Orca* (left) and *Jesse H. Freeman* at Point Barrow a few days before they were trapped and crushed by the ice. (Private Collection)

The *Belvedere* in Seattle, 1913. Built in 1880, the bark made 25 whaling trips
to the Arctic, more than any other steam whaler. In 1919 she was crushed
in the ice off Siberia. (Photography Collection, Suzallo Library, University of Washington,
reprinted from *A Whaler & Trader in the Arctic*)

M.V.B. Millard, master of the *Belvedere*, on hearing about the plight of the ships east of [Point Barrow which were trapped by the ice], provisioned only until January, was persuaded to unload supplies of flour, molasses, coffee, and beans, a gesture displaying both generosity and Millard's belief that he would be released from the ice. As soon as the supplies were unloaded, the three vessels departed south, slowly cutting through the young ice, and by the evening of September 21 they reached Peard Bay, close to open water.[15]

Before the night was out, however, the fate of the vessels had been sealed. A strong northwest wind sprang up at 2 A.M., catching the three in a totally exposed position to which they had worked, about eight miles from Point Belcher. They had nearly reached open water when the first to go, the "*Orca* . . . was caught between two immense ice floes and crushed with such force as to take the stern post and steering gear completely out of her and hurl the wheel through the pilot house. Her officers and crew jumped for the ice immediately."[16]

The *Belvedere* and the *Freeman* were able to get within three-quarters of a mile of the *Orca* and rescued all of her men, but by then escape from the closing ice was impossible. They turned northeast to seek refuge behind Point Franklin. The *Belvedere* under steam and sail succeeded in forcing her way through the thickening ice; however, two hours later the *Freeman* was caught and crushed, and the *Belvedere*, safe behind heavy ground ice at the Sea Horse Islands, took the *Freeman*'s crew aboard as well.[17]

By the time the men had reached the *Belvedere*, the moving pack, driven by a freshening northwesterly, had met the young shore ice, piling and driving it into pressure ridges and cutting off any chance of escape.[18] It must have been tantalizing for the *Belvedere*'s crew and for her one hundred and two passengers who could see from her decks open water only a few miles away across the impenetrable ice at Point Franklin.[19] But Captain Millard with his years of experience in the Arctic must have felt that those few miles could have been a thousand; the odds that the ice would slack off so late in the season were very slim indeed. Consequently he took the only prudent course open to him, continuing on to the northeast. He brought the *Belvedere* around the Sea Horse Islands and into the shallow waters of Peard Bay. If any on board doubted the wisdon of this move, Millard was vindicated on the two days following when the icepack, now driven by a screaming northerly, forced ever harder against the shore, grinding and shearing.

There was no time to lose. Provisions had to be salvaged and the *Belvedere* had to be made ready to winter. Parties were sent to transfer supplies from the two ships, still held afloat by the pressure of the ice. One group reached the *Orca* but another was unable to get to the *Freeman* because of dangerously thin ice. On the evening of the twenty-fourth all were hoping for another attempt to reach the *Freeman* when the sky lit up to the north. The *Freeman* was afire and burned through the night, down to her waterline. It was learned later that a party of Eskimos had succeeded in reaching the hulk, and in their haste at ransacking her cargo had overturned a lamp, igniting some straw and excelsior.[20]

Millard organized his men to prepare the ship. Her supplies and movable equipment were taken ashore, and her bulkheads were torn out for material to build a supply house on one of the islands, a sound idea in case of fire aboard ship during the winter. Her water was jettisoned, and the hull, now sufficiently lightened, was drawn through a channel cut in the young ice, to a position close under the islands.[21]

Meanwhile, George Fred Tilton, third mate of the *Belvedere*, and Charles Walker, fourth mate of the *Orca*, had been hard at work salvaging supplies from the *Orca*, and had succeeded in getting most of her flour and potatoes and twenty cases of canned meat onto the ice. Suddenly they felt her hull shudder and they jumped to the ice; the main and mizzen masts collapsed and the hull slowly rolled over, and sank.[22]

With the sinking of the *Orca*, the scenario for the next six months was essentially dictated. Most of the crew of the *Belvedere* would spend the winter aboard their vessel on short rations, as would the crews of the *Rosario*, *Newport*, *Fearless*, and *Jeanie*. But nearly one hundred men from the *Orca* and the *Freeman* would have to make their way sixty miles to Point Barrow and seek refuge there. . . .

FOOTNOTES

1. Brower claimed that the captain had taken the *Navarch* past Icy Cape despite the dangerous ice conditions because his wife, who was with him, so disliked the wife of the master of the steam brigantine *Karluk* that she could not endure the two vessels being close to one another. Accordingly, when the *Karluk* arrived at the *Navarch*'s anchorage south of Icy Cape, Captain Whiteside, to avoid a marital squabble, weighed anchor and took his vessel around Blossom Shoals to the north side of the cape. Charles D. Brower, "The Northernmost American: An Autobiography," undated typescript, Naval Arctic Research Laboratory, Barrow, Alaska, p. 497.
2. *Navarch*, log, 1897, Old Dartmouth Historical Society, New Bedford, Mass. (Unless otherwise noted, the logs hereinafter cited are from this source.)
3. Brower, "Autobiography," pp. 496-497.
4. Norman G. Buxton, manuscript journal, private collection, p. 25.
5. Brower, "Autobiography," p. 500.
6. Ibid., pp. 502-508.
7. *Belvedere*, log (222), 1897-98, pp. 32-35.
8. Ibid., pp. 35-36.
9. *Alexander*, log, 1897-1900, pp. 41-45; Brower, "Autobiography," p. 510; E. A. McIlhenny, manuscript journal, private collection, p. 40.
10. *San Francisco Call*, Nov. 4, 1897.
11. McIlhenny, journal, p. 40.
12. Ibid., pp. 39-40.
13. *Rosario*, log, 1897-98, Dukes County Historical Society, Edgartown, Mass.
14. *Belvedere*, log (222), pp. 36-37; Brower, "Autobiography," p. 510.
15. *Belvedere*, log (545), p. 62; McIlhenny, journal, p. 47.
16. *San Francisco Call*, Apr. 9, 1898.
17. McIlhenny, journal, pp. 55-57.
18. *San Francisco Call*, Apr. 9, 1898.
19. *Belvedere*, log (222), p. 38.
20. Ibid.; Brower, "Autobiography," p. 532.
21. *Belvedere*, log (545), pp. 63-66.
22. Ibid., log (222) p. 39; Buxton, journal, pp. 50-51; *San Francisco Call*, Apr. 9, 1898. □

This 96-foot, 200,000- pound blue whale yielded 200 barrels of oil for whalers at Akutan in the Aleutians. This was an average size whale for the period. (Photography Collection, Suzallo Library, University of Washington)

By LAEL MORGAN

Modern Shore-based Whaling

The crush of the arctic ice pack, which destroyed the great Yankee and San Francisco sail and steam whaling fleets off Alaska's arctic coast, heralded economic doom for Alaska's most romantic whaling era but signaled the beginning of another—that of a modern shore-based industry.

Even before the expense of the great fleets proved unfeasible, hunting whales from a permanent land base was fairly lucrative and with the decline in the market for oil and bone, it became increasingly necessary to sell the entire carcass—meat and bones, as well as blubber and baleen—to make a whaling venture pay. This could not be handled easily by the floating cookeries, most of which were steamers of some 8,000 tons equipped only to render oil, so shore whaling came into its own.

The first operation was established by the Russians at Kodiak probably in the late 1700's. There was still a good market for baleen and oil but the Russians were trying to support a struggling colony and found it necessary to utilize the meat which visiting Yankee whaling fleets generally ignored.

Although this concept was innovative, the method by which the Russians took their whales was anything but innovative. Their budget apparently didn't include the use of sailing ships so they made do with Aleut employees who hunted much in the manner of their ancestors.

Father Gideon, Cathedral Hieromonk of the Alexandro-Nevsky Lavra, writing between 1804 and 1807, reported on whaling at Kodiak.

The [Russian American] Company assigns the best of the Kad'iak inhabitants to hunt whales—about 30 men, who hunt near Kad'iak and Afognak. They are dispatched into various

ABOVE — Headquarters for the thriving shore-based whaling industry in the Aleutians was Akutan, on Akutan Island in the Krenitzin Islands group in the Aleutian Chain. The last season at Akutan was 1939. (Photography Collection, Suzzallo Library, University of Washington)

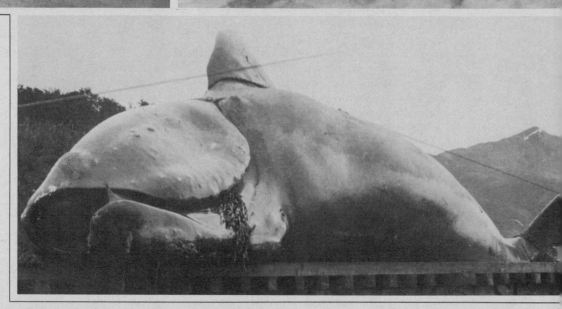

TOP — An 80-foot blue whale lies on a ramp at Sechelt, British Columbia. (Provincial Archives, Victoria, British Columbia)

ABOVE — A fin whale ready for butchering at Akutan in the Aleutians. (Photography Collection, Suzzallo Library, University of Washington)

UPPER RIGHT — Whalers at Akutan gather around a killer whale. (Photography Collection, Suzzallo Library, University of Washington)

RIGHT — A right whale, 15 feet high, 22 feet wide, 65 feet long, and approximately 250 tons, ashore at Port Hobron on the north coast of Sitkalidak Island, southeast of Kodiak Island. (Photography Collection, Suzzallo Library, University of Washington)

36

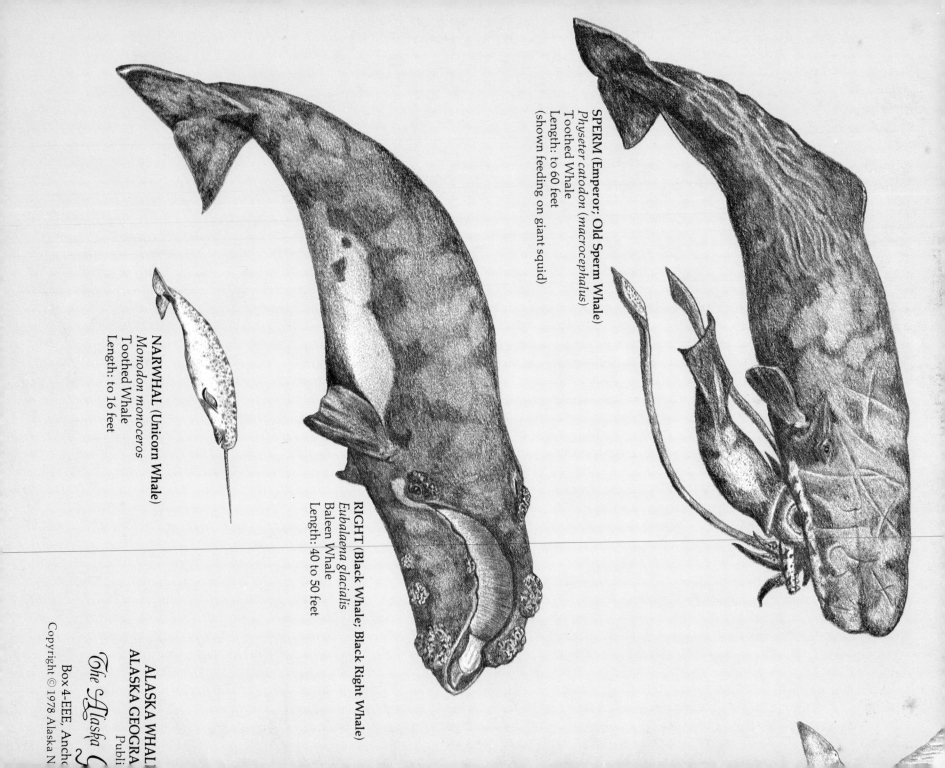

SPERM (Emperor; Old Sperm Whale)
Physeter catodon (macrocephalus)
Toothed Whale
Length: to 60 feet
(shown feeding on giant squid)

NARWHAL (Unicorn Whale)
Monodon monoceros
Toothed Whale
Length: to 16 feet

RIGHT (Black Whale; Black Right Whale)
Eubalaena glacialis
Baleen Whale
Length: 40 to 50 feet

ALASKA WHAL
ALASKA GEOGRA
Publi

The Alaska G
Box 4-EEE, Anch

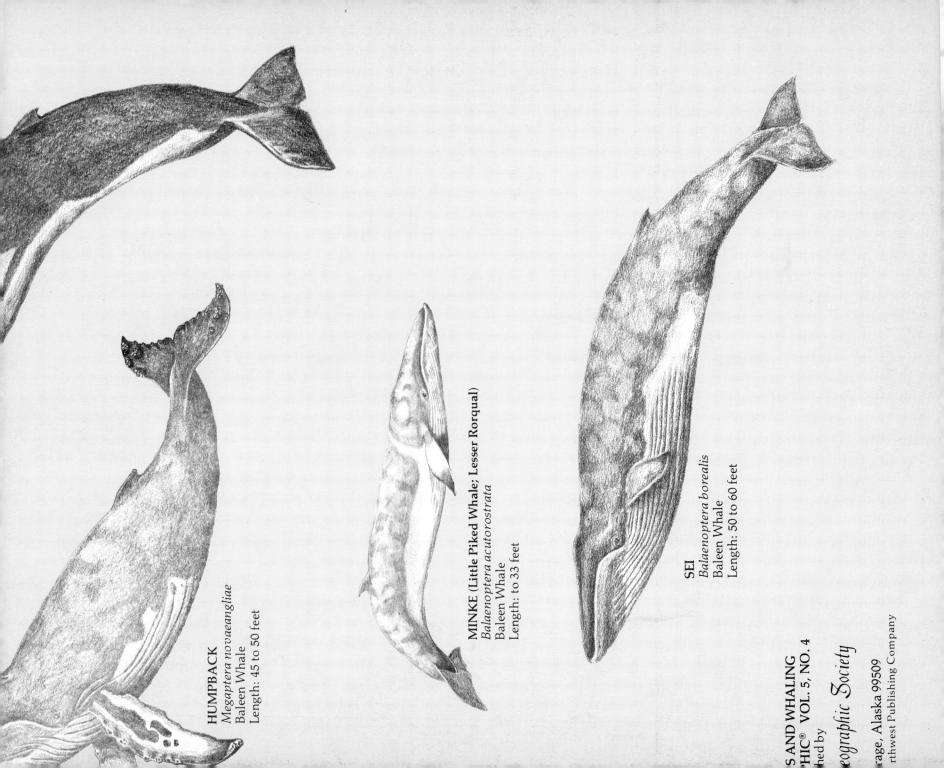

HUMPBACK
Megaptera novaeangliae
Baleen Whale
Length: 45 to 50 feet

MINKE (Little Piked Whale; Lesser Rorqual)
Balaenoptera acutorostrata
Baleen Whale
Length: to 33 feet

SEI
Balaenoptera borealis
Baleen Whale
Length: 50 to 60 feet

S AND WHALING
HIC® VOL. 5, NO. 4
hed by
eographic Society

age, Alaska 99509
rthwest Publishing Company

TOP — The head and mouth of a toothed sperm whale being butchered at Akutan. Early whalers particularly valued sperm whales for their oil and ivory. ABOVE — A minke, one of the smaller baleen whales, laid out on the dock at Akutan. (Both photos from Photography Collection, Suzzallo Library, University of Washington)

bays, by twos and fours, depending on the suitability of the place. The hunters go out singly, in one-hatch bidarkas, and choose yearling whales because their meat and fat are tastier and [more] tender.

Once the hunter observes such an animal, he approaches to the distance of not more than three sazhen [seven feet] and tries to aim his dart under the side flipper then tries to evade with great skill the thrashing beast: the whale can crush the hunter's boat or the wave caused by the diving whale may overturn his bidarka. . . .

Some whale hunters will during the summer season take up to eight whales, rarely 10. Those who kill more than four whales—which is the quota—are paid by the company in goods worth about five rubles.

The hunter whose dart wounded the whale was entitled to the inferior half of the carcass but, according to Father Gideon, the agreement was seldom honored. Most of the meat went for Russian consumption, preserved at the big blubbering station at Three Saints Bay or lesser stations around the island and packed into big storage *barabaras* (sod buildings).

A favorite dish was pavlina—the belly part of a fresh whale steamed in a special way and smeared with fish roe for preservation, then cooked in sourberries (a variety of cranberry) before being packed into barrels. Some 200 puds (one pud equals 36.11 pounds) of pavlina were prepared annually, for Russian use only.

In 1849 the Russian American Company became a partner in a whaling enterprise named the Russian Finland Whaling Company, which was subsidized by the Russian government. Six whaling vessels were fitted out to operate in the Sea of Okhotsk between the Kamchatka Peninsula and the Russian mainland and Bering Sea, where whaling was then dominated by the British and Yankees. The venture was a failure, in part at least because of the Crimean War. Russian whalers could not get to ports where they could sell their catches and one and perhaps more of the vessels was captured by English and French naval vessels.

In 1880 the Northwest Trading Company, which had headquarters at Portland, Oregon, established a trading post on Killisnoo Island in Chatham Strait in Southeastern Alaska. A short while later the company began to kill whales in Kootzna-

The 71-ton killer boat *Tyee Jr.* tows a whale through the waterways of Southeastern Alaska. (Vincent I. Soboleff, courtesy of R. N. De Armond)
INSET — Indiantown at Killisnoo, Alaska. (Seattle Historical Society)

hoo Inlet adjacent to the station and to process the carcasses for oil, bone and fertilizer. The operation was not very successful, perhaps because of inexperienced crews. Two men were killed when a bomb gun exploded and there was difficulty getting a steady supply of whales close to the station. After a few years the company began to harvest herring and abandoned the whaling effort.

In 1907 Tyee Company moved into Murder Cove, Admiralty Island, also in Southeastern Alaska. The venture got off to a slow start when delivery of its whaling steamer was delayed by builders until that first fall and subsequent seasons weren't much better.

"This station was operated in 1908, 1909 and 1910, but . . . the whales were becoming shyer every year and more inclined to keep to the open ocean, thus compelling the whaling vessels to go long distances . . .," *Pacific Fisherman* reported in September 1914. "In 1911 the oil-making machinery was placed aboard a large barge and during the first half of the season whaling was carried on in the neighborhood of Kodiak Island, the catch cut up aboard this barge and the oil tried out. No attempt was made to prepare fertilizer [from the bone] as in previous years. Later in

the season the floating station was towed to Southeast Alaska and operated there. The same method was followed in 1912, the floating station being located in Southeast Alaska, but as the venture had proven not profitable the shore station and vessels were sold in 1913 and the machinery taken to the states."

At its peak, Tyee operated a six-vessel fleet: the killer boat, *Tyee Jr.* (71 tons); the schooner *Allen A* (266 tons); the unrigged vessels *Diamond Head* (952 tons) and *Fresno* (1149 tons); the steamer *Fearless* (85 tons); and the gas schooner *Lizzie S. Sorrenson* (49 tons).

In 1910 a wounded whale rammed the *Sorrenson*, opening a hole in her stern and sinking her eight miles southwest of Cape Addington on Noyes Island in Southeastern Alaska. The crew escaped in small boats and was rescued two days later by the *Fearless*, but things went downhill from there.

The company took 146 whales in 1910 and 218 the following year but it was not enough to cover the large capital investment—now there was competition.

In 1907 Norwegians financed a small whaling venture at Akutan, Aleutian Islands, and with infusion of American capital and incorporation as Alaska Whaling Company in 1912, a sub-

Vera Soboleff standing on a whale near the Killisnoo dock. Whales were stored at Killisnoo while the killer boat *Tyee Jr.* continued to hunt. Later the whales were towed to Murder Cove on Admiralty Island in Southeastern Alaska. (Vincent I. Soboleff, courtesy of R. N. De Armond)

The harpoon gunner is alert as the whaling ship strives to overtake a spouting whale. (Provincial Archives, Victoria, British Columbia)

fishing. At the bow of each is mounted a muzzle-loading whale gun of 3¼-inch bore. These guns are now fitted with recoil cylinders, which is an improvement over the original form of Svend Foyn gun. The charge of black powder is first put in, then a bunch of waste, and next the harpoon, to which is attached the line leading back to the steam winches which are made to play a whale after it is struck, in manner similar to that of an angler who plays his catch. Outside the gun and made a part of the harpoon is a bomb, with expanding arms and so timed as to explode within the whale. The average shooting distance is about 120 feet. In rough weather it is difficult to hit a whale on account of the motion both of the vessel and the animal, and this factor has much to do with the success or failure of whaling operations."

Optimistically, the United States Whaling Company expanded its facility for the 1913 season, enlarging its plant to handle 500 whales and employ 302 hands, but its high hopes were dashed—apparently by rough weather—and the year's catch was only 99 whales.

The company never topped its first year. Its catch, which was 117 in 1914, dropped to a dismal 79 in 1918. In 1919 the count was 102; in 1920 an even 100; and in 1923 United States Whaling called it quits, transferring its gear to New Zealand.

Meanwhile the Akutan operation continued to prosper, perhaps with the help of new capital and some paper shuffling, for it changed names several times, becoming Pacific Sea Products in 1914 and North Pacific Whaling Company in 1915.

Apparently worried about competition, backers of the firm introduced legislation before Congress in 1915 which would have prevented any rival from building within 75 miles of their base. Congress saw through the bill, however, because passage would have given the company a virtual monopoly on whaling in both major passes through the Aleutians. Failure to pass the legislation did not matter though because the competition was already dead.

Remnants of the San Francisco whaling fleet had continued to travel north for a few years after its arctic heyday, but by 1914 the price of baleen had dropped to 75 cents a pound, petroleum had pretty much replaced whale oil and pickings were slim. In 1916 the steamer *Herman* and the auxiliary whaling schooner *Belvedere* sailed north for one more try but it was a dismal season and they didn't return.

stantial shore base was built there. The company lost a chartered bark, *Hadyn Brown*, with several hands early in its first year but managed to take a total of 310 whales which put the venture on sound footing.

Also competing was the United States Whaling Company, established in 1912 at Port Armstrong, about three miles north of Port Alexander near the south end of Baranof Island in Southeastern Alaska. Also Norwegian backed, the operation boasted three killer boats, *Stars 1, 2* and *3*, and topped all records its first year with a catch of 314 whales.

This success, according to an account in *Alaska Fisheries and Fur Industries in 1913*, was due to modern technology:

"The killing boats are the modern type common to whale

LEFT — Captain Larsen of the S.S. *Saint Lawrence* mans the harpoon gun in this 1908 photo taken in the Gulf of Georgia off British Columbia. (Provincial Archives, Victoria, British Columbia)

BELOW — Stanford Professor Harold Heath (second from right) and others examine a dissected whale heart at the Akutan whaling station about 1918. (Courtesy of Dr. Victor B. Scheffer)

"There has been some talk of protecting the whale by law in order to prevent its total extinction," mused Knut Kirkland, president of the Akutan company who eventually wrote *Whalers of Akutan*, (1926) one of the few books available on shore-based whaling. "This is, in my opinion, unnecessary, for the whale protects itself. Years ago anyone with a rifle could kill the last buffalo and make money on it; but no one would be able to capture the last whale without spending several hundred thousand dollars in one season, for the business of modern whaling requires much capital, both for the construction of boats and stations, and for operating expenses. When the number of whales decreases to such an extent that whaling no longer pays, the industry will naturally cease to exist; while there will still be enough whales left to multiply and in later years make it profitable once more for the hunter."

There was a flurry of hope with the establishment of a beluga

The Pacific Steam Whaling Co. office in Nome, Alaska. Here men with their
sleeping rolls and dufflebags awaited passage on steamers to Golovnin Bay,
72 miles east of Nome. For the hungry, meals were 50 cents at the restaurant and
lodging house. (Seattle Historical Society)

industry in Cook Inlet. To catch the belugas a net was stretched across the river with a large rubber tube fastened to its upper edge. During the incoming tide the net was allowed to sink to the bottom. After the belugas had entered the river, the rubber tube was pumped full of air, raising the net to block the river and easily trap the animals, at low tide. Leather from the small, white whales was in demand for gloves and in 1915 J. A. Magill, a salmon salter from Anchorage, established the first beluga industry with his gas boat *Magna*.

The company was incorporated in 1916 as Beluga Whaling Company and in 1917 was listed as having capital investment of $39,935 with 12 employees. The take, according to a 1918 report, was 41 beluga hides valued at $1,250. Three sperm whales were also listed in the catch records for that year. The firm isn't mentioned again until 1920 when, under the name J. A. Magill and Co., Beluga River, it reported its most successful season—100 belugas taken. The company then disappeared entirely from record.

A similar undertaking, Beluga Whaling Company, was listed in Nome in 1917 with no catch given; and in 1919 Pioneer Mining and Dutch Company of Nome took 41 beluga skins. The company was not mentioned in records for the following years. The final reference to any commercial beluga whaling effort was the report of an Arctic Whaling and Fish Company, Golovnin Bay, which took 136 small whales in 1920 and was not heard from thereafter.

Actually the whaling industry went out to sea again with the invention of the stern slipway in 1925 which enabled whalers to haul whole carcasses aboard a factory ship, thus permitting them to operate on the high seas and freeing them from regulation by national governments.

Stubbornly the whalers of Akutan hung on to their shore base, taking 100 or so whales a year there and even expanding their operation about 1917 to Port Hobron, on Sitkalidak Island off Kodiak Island until the long shadows of World War II sent them back to their native Norway.

The last season in Akutan was 1939 and shortly thereafter their plant was leased to the U.S. Navy which rebuilt the wobbly dock and used it for refueling Russian freighters. At the war's end the property was returned to its original owners but the processing plant—outdated and rusty—burned to the ground. □

LEFT — Tooth of a sperm whale saved by a workman from the Bay City, Washington, whaling station sometime between 1911 and 1925. (Dr. Victor B. Scheffer) BELOW — The whaling steamer, *Saint Lawrence.* (Photography Collection, Suzzallo Library, University of Washington)

43

Alaska Natives cut up a whale in the water through young ice. (The University Museum, Pennsylvania)

INSET — The frame of a skin boat (*umiak*) rests on supports at Saint Lawrence Island. Normally the frame is made of driftwood, which is lightweight, durable and easy to carry over the ice floes. (Phyllis Mithassel, reprinted from *ALASKA*® magazine)

Early Native Whaling in Alaska

By LAEL MORGAN

ALTHOUGH THE ONLY ALASKAN WHALING CULTURE which survives today is that of the northern Eskimo, there were many Native whaling cults along the coasts before the coming of the white man. Baron von Wrangell, Russian American Company manager from 1830 to 1835, reported that the Kenai and Tanaina Indians of Cook Inlet did not hunt whales, supposedly because they were inland people and only newly arrived to the coast. However, in *The Archaeology of Cook Inlet, Alaska* (1934) anthropologist Frederica de Laguna states that Alec Mishikof, a Kenai Indian, told her that the Kenais had rock shelters around Kachemak Bay that were "secret places where the whalers used to boil out the human fat from which they made poison for their lance blades. Afterwards the bones had to be reassembled (with pitch, he hazarded) and fed regularly, otherwise the skeleton would pursue the whaler and devour him." Anthropologists speculate these rock shelters may well have been made by early Eskimos who preceded the Indians to this region and were forced out by them.

Farther south the majority of Tlingit Indians also abstained from whaling, perhaps because their forests were rich with game that was easier to obtain or maybe, as von Wrangell suggests, because they, too, were relatively new to the coast.

The only exception among the Tlingits were the people of Yakutat who did pursue the great whales. According to an account published in 1801 (*A Voyage round the World performed during the years 1790, 1791, 1792 by Etienne Marchand*) "[the Yakutat Tlingits] use a barbed bone harpoon with a long shaft. When they come to the spot where they last saw [the whale] dive, they slow up their boats and play slowly on the surface of the water with their paddles and as soon as [the whale] appears, the harpooner reaches for his harpoon and throws it at the monster."

The Eskimos of Little Diomede Island, although still dedicated subsistence hunters, do not take whale today. Apparently though, Eskimos of both Little and Big Diomede Islands were once steeped in a strong whaling tradition. A local teacher, E.W. Hawkes, reported strong evidence of this in a letter to the University of Pennsylvania Museum in 1916. His find [which he was trying to sell the museum] was "a complete whaling outfit belonging to the rough stone age. It was the custom at that time for a famous whaler to leave behind him a collection of his implements, fetishes and a record in

ABOVE — Kodiak Island Natives attack a whale with poison lances as reported in an account published in 1844 by the French explorer de Mofras. (Reprinted from *The ALASKA SPORTSMAN*®)

An Eskimo graveyard at Point Hope on the Chukchi Sea coast is fringed with the bones of whales. (Lael Morgan, Staff, reprinted from *A Whaler & Trader in the Arctic*)

ivory of his prowess as a hunter. So ancient, however, [was] the tradition that no such collection was ever among the present generation."

Margaret Lantis in *The Alaskan Whale Cult and Its Affinities* (1938) also documents the whaling past of the people of the Diomede Islands. According to her research, those whaling crews were comprised of the sturdiest and bravest men of the village. The people, who also were famous for tattooing, "added a tattooed dot above the upper lip for every whale killed."

It was the Aleuts, however, who showed themselves to be formidable whale hunters. William H. Dall, excavating on the Aleutians in 1887, found remains of killer whales, bowheads, right whales, grays, fins and sperms in ancient garbage pits. The work of other archaeologists bears him out.

Aleut hunting techniques, according to Veniaminov who wrote from Unalaska from 1824 to 1834 (Petroff translation, 1884), were quite different from those in the north.

> The pursuit of whales was encumbered with many observances and superstitions. The spear-heads used in hunting the whale were greased with human fat, or portions of human bodies were tied to them, obtained from corpses found in burial caves. . . . The hunters who obtain such charms are always fortunate in their pursuit, but meet with an untimely and painful death. . . . All such objects had their own special properties and influence, and the whalers always kept them in their bidarkas. The hunter who launched a spear provided with such a charm upon a whale at once blew upon his hands, and having sent one spear and struck the whale, he would not throw again, but would proceed at once to his home, separate himself from his people in a specially constructed hovel, where he remained 3 days without food or drink, and without touching or looking upon a female. During this time of seclusion he snorted occasionally in imitation of the wounded and dying whale, in order to prevent the whale struck by him from leaving the coast. On the fourth day he emerged from his seclusion and bathed in the sea, shrieking in a hoarse voice and beating the water with his hands.

In another account of early Native whaling, Father Gideon, Cathedral Hieromonk of the Alexandro-Nevsky Lavra, wrote that "the whale hunters used to

Wainwright whalers butcher a
53-foot, 6-inch bowhead taken by
Felton Segevan's crew in the spring
1978 hunt. The whale contained a
2-foot fetus. (Lael Morgan, Staff,
reprinted from *ALASKA®*
magazine)
INSET — From left: A shoulder gun,
darting gun and harpoon with float.
(Lael Morgan, Staff)

A whaling camp on an ice lead. (Lael Morgan, Staff, reprinted from *A Whaler & Trader in the Arctic*)

secretly disinter dead bodies, carry the remains into the mountains and render from these bodies fat to smear the points of their whale arrows. For this purpose they also gathered worms from the dead bodies, secretly dried them and attached them to whaling arrows."

Dr. Henry Collins, an archaeologist at the Smithsonian Institution reported the poison used was probably an extract from the roots of monkshood, which was common in the area and widely used on the Asian coast.

As for the hunt itself, two *bidarkas* usually went out together so that if one overturned by violent thrashing from the wounded whale, the other came to the rescue, Dr. Collins reported in *The Aleutian Islands: Their People and Natural History* (1945). Approaching from the rear, hunters cast their spears rapidly and retreated. The harpoon head detached and in about three days the animal died. The harpoon head bore the owner's mark and if he was lucky enough for the whale to drift ashore, cutting the flesh away from the wound would prevent the poison from affecting the people.

Perhaps the Aleuts' passion for whaling discouraged other Native people to the south. According to Dr. Victor Scheffer who surveyed whaling off the state of Washington in the middle 1940's, "Natives of the coast between the Gulf of Alaska and Vancouver Island were not whalers [except for the Yakutat people] and some even refused to eat the flesh of whales found stranded on the beach, possibly as the result of unhappy experience with poisoned carcasses which drifted down to them from the Aleut-Koniag region." □

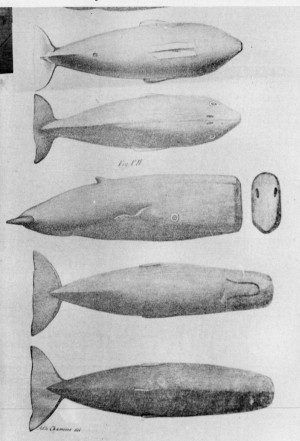

These Aleut renditions of whale species in the waters off the Aleutians were first published in Bonn, Germany, in 1824. The carvings were done to describe the whales to an explorer who came through the Aleuts' territory in the 1700's. (Reprinted from Verh. Kaiserlichen Leopoldinisch-Carolinishnen Akad. Natur forsch.)

WHALE DISTRIBUTION IN EARLIER TIMES

The map at right shows the distribution of northern and southern right whales based on logbook records of whaling ships, collected from 1785 to 1913, and representing catches of 8,415 right whales. The map was prepared under the direction of Charles Haskins Townsend and is reprinted here from *Zoologica*, Vol. XIX, No. 1, April 3, 1935, with permission of the New York Zoological Society.

KEY TO DISTRIBUTION MAP — NORTHERN AND SOUTHERN RIGHT WHALES

The colored dots represent the position of a whaling ship on the day when at least one whale was taken.

January - Black (solid)

February - Yellow (open)

March - Yellow (solid)

April - Green (open)

May - Green (solid)

June - Blue (open)

July - Blue (solid)

August - Red (open)

September - Red (solid)

October - Brown (open)

November - Brown (solid)

December - Black (open)

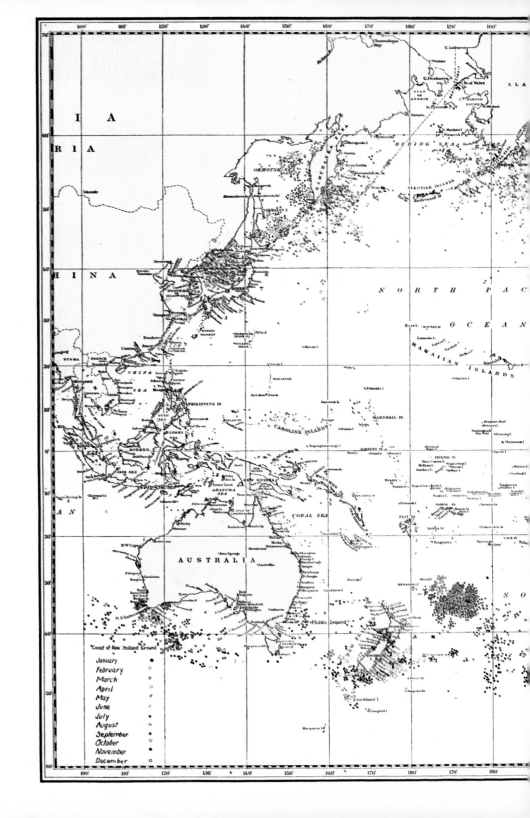

PLATE III

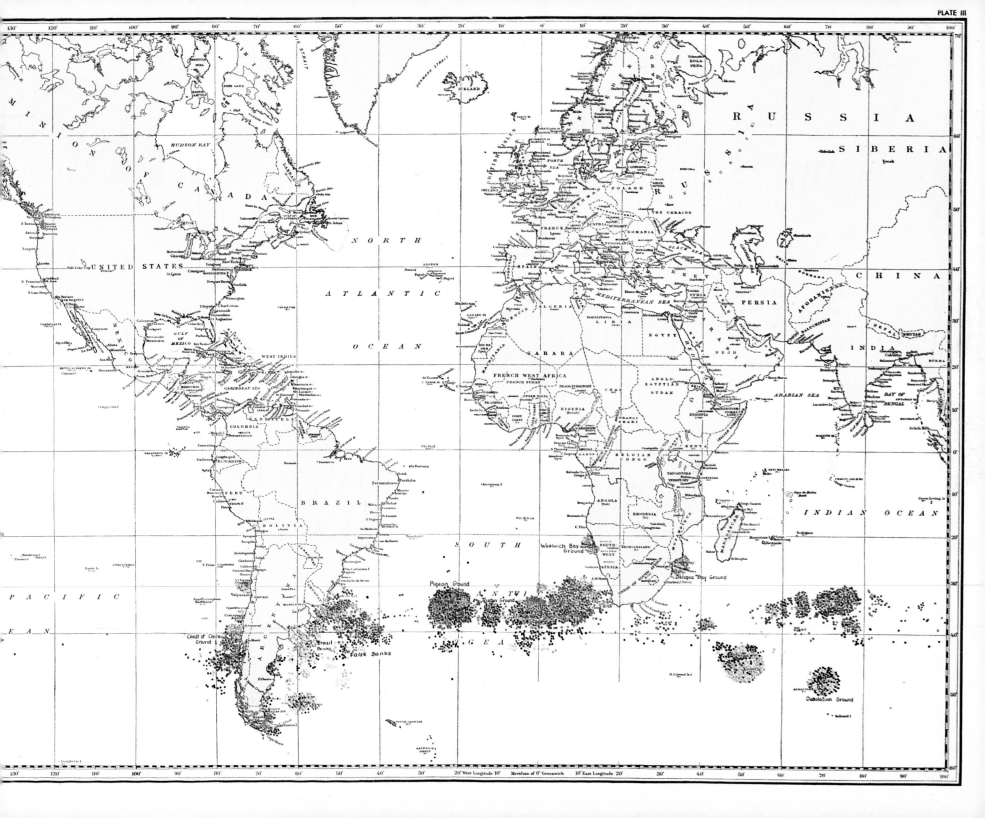

WHALE DISTRIBUTION IN EARLIER TIMES

The map at right shows distribution of bowhead and humpback whales based on logbook records, mostly from the 19th century, and representing catches of 5,114 bowhead and 2,883 humpback whales. The map was prepared under the direction of Charles Haskins Townsend and is reprinted here from *Zoologica*, Vol. XIX, No. 1, April 3, 1935, with permission of the New York Zoological Society.

KEY TO DISTRIBUTION MAP — BOWHEAD AND HUMPBACK WHALES

The colored dots represent the position of a whaling ship on the day when at least one whale was taken.

January - Black (solid)

February - Yellow (open)

March - Yellow (solid)

April - Green (open)

May - Green (solid)

June - Blue (open)

July - Blue (solid)

August - Red (open)

September - Red (solid)

October - Brown (open)

November - Brown (solid)

December - Black (open)

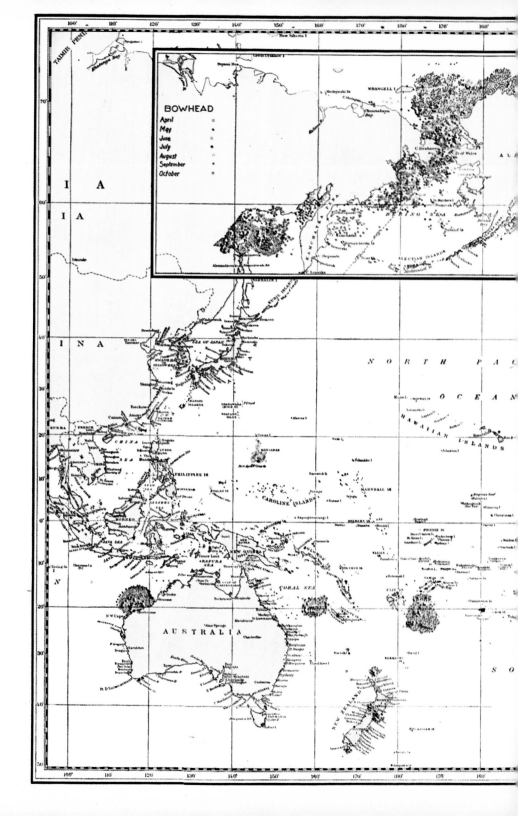

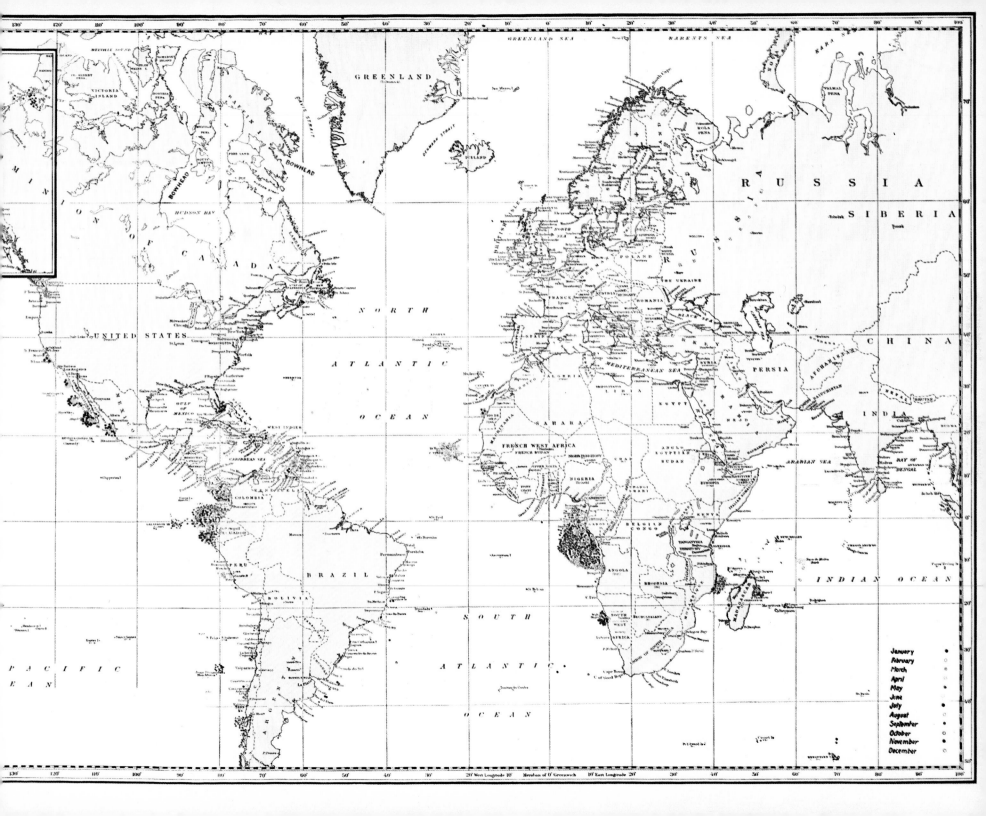

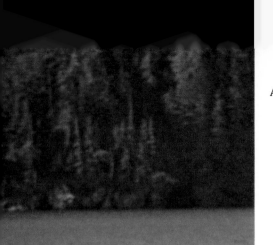

Kayakers paddle between two humpbacks near Chenega Island, southeast of Whittier in the western portion of Prince William Sound. (John Hall)

GLOSSARY

Amphipod
A marine crustacean, usually 1 to 2 inches long, whose body has been compressed sideways to give it a shrimplike appearance. Most amphipods are transparent or gray, but they can vary from brown and red, to green or blue-green. Gammarus and parathemisto seem to be the most common amphipods used for food by whales in Alaskan waters. Benthic amphipods are those which live on, just above or just below the ocean floor.

Annelid Worms
Segmented worms. Polychaete worms are annelid worms living in a marine environment. Some polychaetes are carried about by the ocean currents and some are sessile. Eskimos have reported that bowheads seem to feed on pelagic forms of polychaetes near the surface, especially in the spring.

Balaenid
Baleen whales with no grooves flowing from their lower jaw.

Balaenopterid
Baleen whales with grooves flowing from their lower jaw backwards along the ventral surface of their bodies.

Baleen
Triangular horny plates with fringed or frayed inner margins which hang from the upper palate of baleen whales and are used to filter out fish and marine invertebrates.

Breaching
An action where whales leap above the surface of the water.

Callosity
An irregular protuberance of horny material on the rostrum of the right whale.

Copepods
A small subclass of crustaceans which make up a major portion of the pelagic marine food web. Copepods are more abundant in temperate and tropical waters than in frigid waters and most baleen whales feed on them.

Dorsal Surface
A whale's back or upper side. The dorsal fin is the single fin located along the back of some whales.

Echolocation
A system by which a whale establishes location of objects by determining the amount of time needed for an echo to return and the direction in which it returns. Echolocation is associated primarily with toothed whales.

Euphausiids
Shrimplike crustaceans which are usually pelagic and about 1 inch long. Euphausiids are a major food source for baleen whales.

Fluke
The expanded flat portion at the tip of a whale's tail.

Krill
A food source for whales. Krill is usually associated with euphausiids but more and more the term is taking on the general meaning of food, especially for the baleen whales.

Rorqual
Any whales of the genus *Balaenoptera*, i.e., those whales with grooves on their ventral surface.

Rostrum
The forward extension of the upper jaw of a whale.

Spy Hopping
An action of a whale of holding its body in a vertical position with its head out of the water, presumably to look around.

Tubercles
Small projections or bumps on the snout, chin and lips of some whales, especially the humpback.

Ventral Surface
The underside of a whale.

Vibrissae
Stiff hairs, like whiskers, which grow near the mouths of some whales. □

Alaska's Whales
A Closer Look

Drawings for this section by DONALD SINETI

We have concentrated, in the following pages, on the 15
species of whales that occur in Alaskan waters and have
outlined their distribution, behavior and physical characteristics.
Experts are still debating the scientific names of some cetaceans
and we've chosen to follow the guidelines of the Marine Mammal
Commission. Intensive study of whales is being carried out by private
citizens and by all levels of government but there is still much to learn.
Population estimates of whales are constantly changing and knowledge
about their behavior and distribution is perpetually being refined. The
glossary of some of the common scientific terms associated with whales will
help you more fully enjoy this closer look at Alaska's whales.

ABOVE — This minke breached several
times in Ugak Bay off Kodiak Island.
(Daniel H. Wieczorek)

55

Right whales are the temperate-water relatives of the bowheads and, although they are scarce, right whales are believed to feed in the Gulf of Alaska and in the waters off the eastern Aleutians.

Right

Eubalaena glacialis

The right whale is also called the black whale, black right whale or Biscayan right whale. And in some books this species is confused with the bowhead, which is also known as the Greenland right whale.

The right whale, however, is a distinctly different species having slightly shorter baleen plates than the bowhead and a head with conspicuous callosities which are sometimes covered with lice and barnacles. The right whale also is found mainly in temperate waters of the Atlantic and Pacific Oceans while the bowhead is found primarily in polar waters.

If they follow the routes of their ancestors, the Pacific stocks of the right whales spend the summer in the rich waters from Vancouver Island off British Columbia, Canada, to the Kodiak grounds, throughout the Gulf of Alaska and the eastern Aleutians. Their wintering grounds are unknown though individuals have been seen off La Jolla, California and off Baja California. Dr. Raymond M. Gilmore, Natural History Museum, San Diego, who has tracked the Atlantic stock of the right whale, has not been successful in learning where the Pacific's right whale stocks winter. "I've combed the coast for them," he admits in exasperation, "but the weather is a lot worse in the Pacific. If I could go back, I know I'd find them."

Right whales feed on copepods which they catch with 230 pairs of baleen plates six to nine feet long.

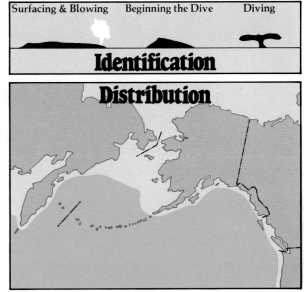

Identification

Distribution

ABOVE — A portion of the head and the tips of the flukes are shown in this photo of a right whale.
BELOW — Right whales characteristically have callosities, irregular mounds of horny material which build up on the rostrum of this species. (Both photos by Aaron Avellar)

From a distance a right whale may be identified by its distinctive double spouts which are exhaled through two well-separated blowholes. Its rostrum is curved, narrow and capped with a large terminal callosity called the bonnet. Like the bowhead, the right whale has no dorsal fin and its body is all black or charcoal gray except for a white region of varying size on its underparts. Unlike the bowhead, the right whale is frequently covered with whale lice and sometimes with barnacles. The right whale averages 40 to 50 feet in length.

Right whales often peer out of the water in a head-up position known as spy hopping. They have also been seen standing on their heads, tails out of the water. What this behavior actually signifies is still being studied, but some scientists believe it may have something to do with feeding. Right whales are also capable of heaving their giant bulks almost clear of the water when breaching.

Right whales were once abundant, but they were nearly wiped out by the turn of the 20th century and only one was reported in California catches after 1918. Right whales were granted protection in 1932 and their numbers may be on the rise in some places. Current world population is estimated at 1,000 to 4,000, with fewer than 300 thought to be in eastern North Pacific waters. □

61

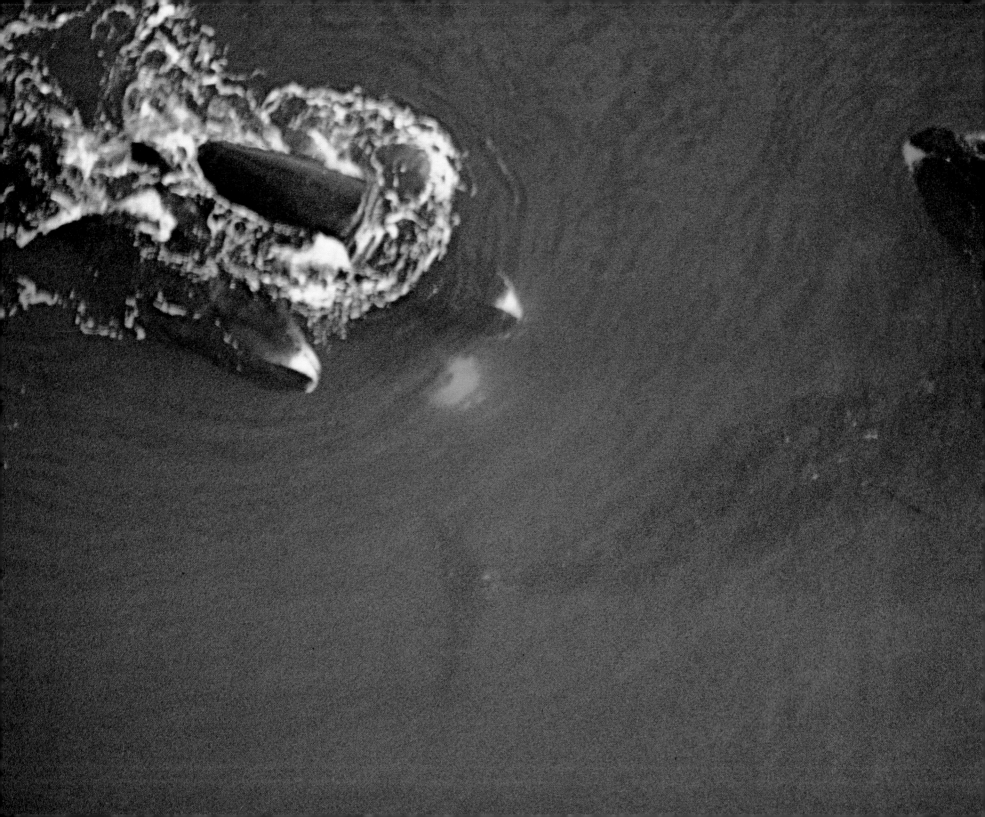

Bowhead

Balaena mysticetus

The bowhead is also known as the Great Polar Whale, Ice Whale, or Greenland Right Whale. It is rich in baleen and oil; slow and easy to catch; and floats when killed which allows easy recovery. To early-day commercial whalers the bowhead was referred to as the Whale because in the North Atlantic, where their efforts were focused, this species was *the* whale to be taken.

The modern wintering grounds of the bowhead have yet to be determined but old whaling records suggest that

they are probably in the southwest Bering Sea near the ice front, mostly in Soviet waters. From early in April through most of May the animals steam past Saint Lawrence Island and on through Bering Strait into the Chukchi Sea where they are anxiously awaited by Eskimo hunters from

Gambell, Savoonga, Kivalina, Point Hope, Wainwright and Barrow. Some, perhaps most, of the species migrate northeast, primarily through near shore leads in the ice pack, across the Beaufort Sea to Banks Island, Canada. According to Stephen Leatherwood, Naval Ocean Systems Center (NOSC),

Belugas are frequently seen with bowheads as the larger whales migrate to the north.

Several bowheads churn the waters of the Bering Sea just north of Big Diomede Island in the Bering Strait. Three animals are swimming toward the lower right corner of the photo and two more whales are circling, one toward the upper right and one toward the upper left. (Dave Withrow, National Marine Fisheries Service)

those bowheads which migrate into the Beaufort Sea appear to expand their range as the ice recedes, entering Amundsen Gulf in the Canadian Arctic as early as July and spreading out along the Arctic coast of Canada and Alaska through September or October. Other bowheads may remain in Chukchi waters or possibly turn northwest toward the Siberian coast. There is no official data to show a spring migration into the western Chukchi Sea, but according to Dr. Howard Braham, Marine Mammal Division, National Marine Fisheries Service, it is perhaps possible for the animals to make a spring migration through this area. A major obstacle for this movement is the thick pack ice which usually covers the western Chukchi Sea but the bowheads could possibly use widely spaced cracks or holes in the ice to reach air. It is also possible that some bowheads may migrate into the Chukchi Sea from the Bering Sea in June, July and August. Of those whales that follow this pattern, it is probable that some do spend time in the western Chukchi area.

Migration patterns for the bowhead are still being studied, but a possible route for the return migration in the fall is for the bowheads in the Beaufort Sea to move westward along the Alaska coast past Point Barrow. From there they head toward Wrangel Island

Chunks of ice surround this pair of copulating bowheads photographed near Point Barrow, Alaska. (Jack W. Lentfer)

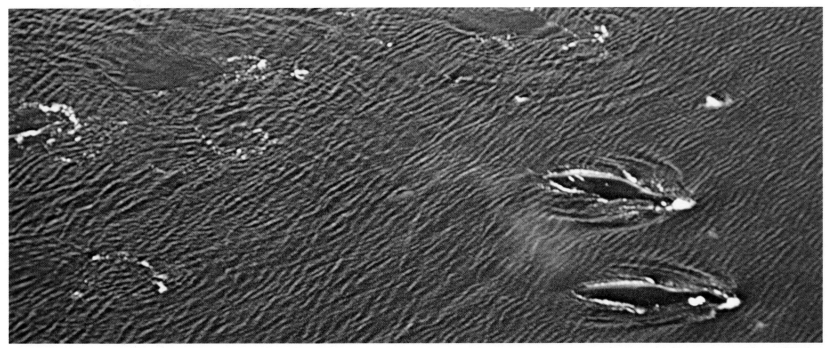

and swim south along the Russian coast to some unknown location.

Little is known about the feeding habits of bowheads but the few samples of stomach contents which have been taken, show that their diet includes annelid worms, amphipods and especially euphausiids. They strain their food from the water with the hairy fringes of up to 600 baleen plates. The bowhead's baleen plates are the longest of any whale species with some reaching 12 feet or more in length.

As a rule of thumb, bowheads weigh a ton a foot and can reach 60 feet in length. Once in a while even longer specimens are recorded. Simeon Patkotak of Barrow took one reported to have measured 67 feet in 1970, Amos Lane of Point Hope recorded a 64-foot bowhead in 1964 and the log of a Yankee whaler reported a 67-foot animal in 1813.

Some Eskimos maintain there is a smaller arctic whale that is sometimes mistaken for the bowhead, but which has a flat, bowless head, hard ribs and jaw bones and a thinner, shorter baleen. This smaller, brownish marine mammal is also distinguished by a rotund body, narrow tail stock, and thicker, sweeter blubber which is so

The dorsal surface of a bowhead is smooth, usually dark colored, and lacks a dorsal fin. (Leslie Nakashima)

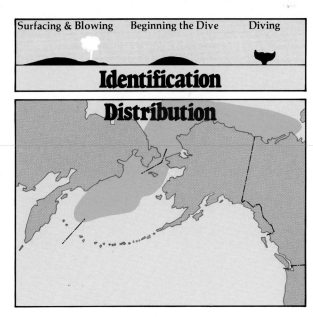

Surfacing & Blowing   Beginning the Dive   Diving

Identification

Distribution

65

tender it can't be pulled by a blubber hook. In cross section the animal's back has an indentation in the center which holds water after it surfaces. Although there is a specific word for this whale in the Eskimo language *inutuq*, scientists to date have recognized no such subspecies.

The bowhead is black, dark brown or dark gray and usually has white marks on the chin and undersides and on the tail. The head of this species makes up one-third of its bulk and its name is derived from a side profile in which arched jaws create the contour of a bowed head. This species lacks a dorsal fin, a characteristic which facilitates swimming under heavy arctic ice. It is commonly speculated that the bowhead uses its baleen-reinforced head as a battering ram when they need to break a hole in the ice to reach air although there is little more than anecdotal evidence to support this.

When migrating, bowheads swim at about four knots if their path is not obstructed by ice. They may be capable of higher speeds when disturbed. Bowheads normally dive for less than six minutes; however, wounded whales have remained under water at least 56 minutes, Eskimos report that this species is adept at swimming bottom side up.

Understandably, bowheads are shy of man but enjoy their own company and, like all whales, they are extremely attached to their young . . . a fact long noted in Eskimo legend and reported in detail by William Scoresby, a Scottish whaling captain and naturalist who hunted the bowhead:

> In June, 1811, one of my Harpooners struck a suck, with the hope of leading to the capture of the mother. . . . Presently she arose close to the "fastboat"; and seizing the young one, dragged about a hundred fathoms of line out of the boat with remarkable force and velocity. Again she arose to the surface; darted furiously to and fro; repeatedly stopped short or suddenly changed her direction, and gave every possible imitation of extreme agony. For a length of time, she continued thus to act, though closely pursued by the boats; and, inspired with courage and resolution by her concern for her offspring, seemed regardless of the danger which surrounded her. At length, one of the boats approached so near that a harpoon was hove at her. It hit, but did not attach itself. A second harpoon was struck; this also failed to penetrate; but a third was more effectual and held. Still she did not attempt to escape; but allowed other boats to approach; so that, in a few minutes three more harpoons were fastened; and in the course of an hour afterwards she was killed.

Until recently it was thought that the bowhead migrated to arctic waters simply to feed. However, recent photos taken by Bruce Krogman, Marine Mammal Division, National Marine Fisheries Service in the southern Chukchi Sea, lead scientists to believe the mammals also mate in the North and perhaps give birth to some of their young there.

The bowhead was a prime quarry of the whaling industry that began in Spitsbergen in 1611 and the quest for this species gradually expanded to Greenland, Baffin Island, the northern

Pacific Ocean and the Sea of Okhotsk between the Kamchatka Peninsula and the Soviet mainland. Bowheads were presumed to be exterminated in the North Atlantic at the turn of the century; however, four were taken by whaling ships off Spitsbergen in 1932 and others have occasionally been sighted.

The Bering Sea bowhead stock was discovered by commercial whalers in 1849 and proved profitable for about the next 60 years. The animal was found to produce more baleen than

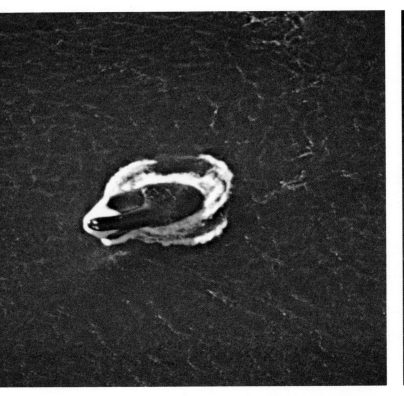
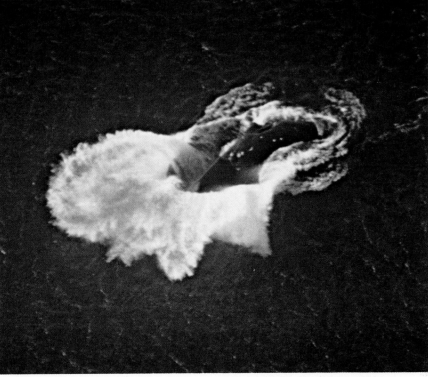

any other—an average of 1,500 pounds per whale—and about 100 barrels of oil. Only a decline in the value of these products spared the creature from extinction.

Bowheads were completely protected from commercial whaling by international regulation in 1946 and subsequently by the Marine Mammal Protection Act of 1972, which made an exception for aboriginal hunters.

Pacific Ocean stocks of the bowhead were reported in the early 1970's to be from "a few hundred" to about 4,000.

The original population, before commercial whaling, was established at 16,000; however Congress has requested reassessment of this figure and in the spring of 1978 personnel at the National Oceanic and Atmospheric Administration projected a total bowhead population of 2,264.

Research on the bowhead has intensified greatly in 1978. Perhaps this increased study with refined techniques will lead to greater understanding of bowhead behavior so that the survival of the species can be guaranteed. □

The bowhead is capable of heaving its massive bulk out of the water when breaching. In this photo sequence taken just south of Little Diomede Island, the whale first thrusts its head out of the water (the dark area is the whale's dorsal surface, the light area its ventral surface), then turns onto its left side, and finally returns to the water with a big splash. (All photos by Stephen Leatherwood, Naval Ocean Systems Center)

A pod of sperm whales.
Females and young can be
seen swimming in groups.
Males without harems do
swim together but tend to
be more solitary.
(Dale W. Rice, NMFS)

Sperm

Physeter catodon (macrocephalus)

Old-time whalers honored the sperm whale with the nickname "Emperor," or "Old Sperm Whale," because this largest of the toothed whales was highly valued for its enormous ivory teeth and unusually fine oil.

In the North Pacific, sperm whales can generally be found south of 40° north, the latitude of northern California, in winter. Breeding groups congregate off the continental slopes of California and in lesser numbers off Baja California and Mexico. In summer, male sperms head north to waters off Southeastern Alaska and the Aleutians. A few animals work their way through the passes in the Aleutians and enter the Bering Sea. Female sperms are seldom, if ever, seen in waters north of 50° N latitude. They apparently prefer to remain in more temperate waters with their young while the males make the long migration to the north.

Sperms feed chiefly on medium-sized and large squid, cuttlefish and octopus although whole sharks and fishermen's boots have been found in their stomachs.

A short blow, normally lower than 8 feet, and definitely angled to the left is characteristic of the sperm whale. (Dale W. Rice, NMFS)

Sperms are the largest of the toothed whales but in feeding they commonly grasp their prey—squid, in this case—and swallow it whole.

69

At sexual maturity a sperm has 18 to 25 teeth, which may measure 3 to 8 inches, on each side of its lower jaw and a few vestigial teeth on its upper jaw. The lower teeth are thought to attract squid with their gleam.

The square-nosed sperm whale is the easiest of all whales to identify. Like the bowhead, its head comprises nearly one-third of its total length; its brain is the largest of any living creature. The large head cavity also contains liquid wax (similar in appearance to semen, hence the name sperm), which is prized as a high-quality industrial lubricant and for making smokeless candles. Scientists speculate that this oil may serve the whale in echolocating and perhaps aid in diving.

The single blowhole of the sperm whale is located well to the left of the midline on the back and far forward on the head. When blowing, the animal produces a single oblique spout which angles forward. Its dorsal fin resembles a corner attached to the back and just behind the fin is a series of scallops leading back to the tail. The skin of the sperm is uniformly rippled, brownish gray with a lighter color on the belly and chin.

The sperm whale cruises easily between three and four knots and can accelerate to 26 knots when threatened. Even more remarkable, however, is the sperm's diving capability. A sperm whale can easily remain submerged for 30 to 60 minutes. The record depth for a whale was set by an unfortunate sperm that got tangled in a submarine cable off the coast of South

TOP — A sperm whale rests near the surface near Ketchikan in Southeastern Alaska. (Alan R. Crane, reprinted from *ALASKA*® magazine)
ABOVE — The flukes of the sperm are broad and thick and show prominently when the animal sounds. (K. C. Balcomb)
OPPOSITE — Dark brownish gray is normal coloring for the sperm. (Dale W. Rice, NMFS)

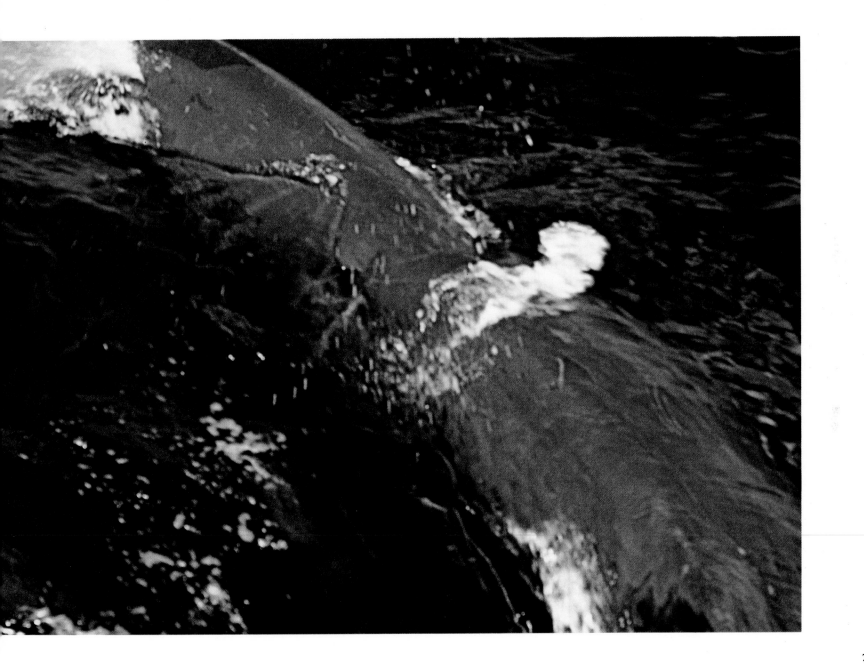

The dorsal hump of the sperm whale usually is rounded and protrudes about two-thirds of the way between the tip of the snout and the tail. (Dale W. Rice, NMFS)

Sperm whales have been hunted for their oil and ivory. Today they are among the more sought after of the great whales. (Dale W. Rice, NMFS)

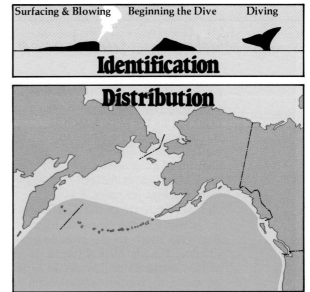

Surfacing & Blowing   Beginning the Dive   Diving

Identification

Distribution

America and died 3,720 feet below the surface.

A sperm whale can be aggressive. In a well-documented case, the 238-ton Nantucket whaler *Essex* was rammed twice and sunk by a sperm whale off South America in 1820.

The sperm and killer whales are the only known polygamous species among the whales but, although they fight for harems and live in a highly gregarious fashion, they have a definite sense of family. Parents have been known to rescue offspring by carrying them in their mouths and a cow sperm is thought to nurse her calf for as long as 16 months.

Early whalers regarded the sperm whale as second in value only to the bowhead because of its oil and ivory.

The species was pursued vigorously during the 18th and 19th centuries and again following World War II. Only recently has a viable substitute for sperm oil, a highly heat resistant lubricant and a base for antibiotics, been discovered. Another by-product of the sperm whale, ambergris, is still highly valued as a perfume base.

Of all whale populations, that of the sperm seems to be the strongest: about 700,000 in the North Pacific, down from an estimated 1 million before intensive commercial whaling began after World War II. Some scientists, however, question these figures and point out that the average weight of the male sperm whale caught in the fishery has dropped about 50%, the result of taking younger individuals.   □

Gray whales have come under more scrutiny than most species of large whales because they migrate close to shore along the Pacific Coast of the United States. (John Kroeger)

shallow water, with its flukes above the surface, and, in an action called spy hopping, raises its head out of water as if to peer at intruders. A few scientists have speculated that both behaviors may have something to do with feeding, but spy hopping also occurs when an animal is clearly not feeding.

Grays have been tracked with radio transmitters diving to depths of 558 feet. Studies continue on the length of time a gray whale can remain submerged, but some scientists believe the whale may be able to stay underwater for longer than 16 minutes.

Of the large whales, the gray is not a particularly fast swimmer. Speeds average four and a half knots during migration with spurts to 11 knots under stress.

Scientists know more about the behavior of grays than other large whales because in migration grays often swim fairly close to shore, making it easy to watch them, and because they breed in shallow lagoons readily accessible to man. In 1971 biologists captured a gray whale calf, perhaps six weeks old, in such a lagoon. Named Gigi, she was raised successfully in captivity and released a year later, in March 1972, equipped with a radio tracking device. Gigi has reportedly been sighted at various times since her release, but

scientists are still considering the validity of these sightings.

Grays usually migrate in small groups of less than 10 (commonly one to three) but 1,000 or more will crowd into a 30-mile breeding lagoon after the trip south.

Mating of gray whales has been described as a "uniquely civilized act." "Two males swim in pursuit of the female . . .," wrote Neil Morgan, of the *San Diego Evening Tribune* in 1978. "But only one prevails. The other male assists in holding the two together during the act and appears to swim in their company afterward for several hours before moving off toward a

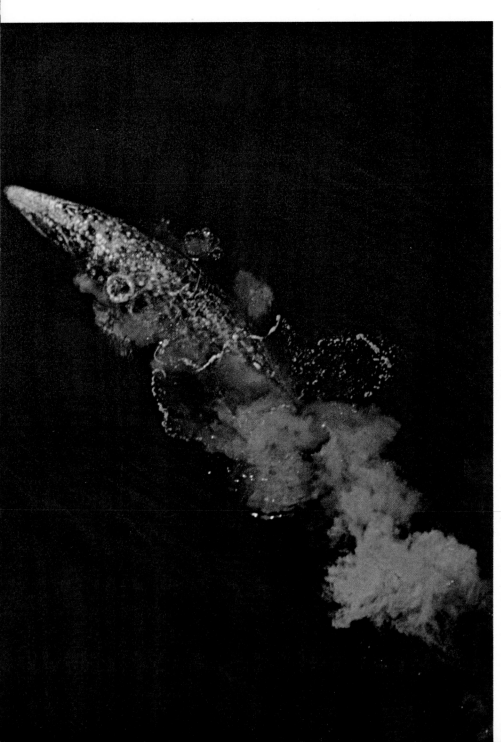

LEFT — Mud from the ocean floor trails along behind a feeding gray whale. Grays stir up the surface of the ocean floor and suck up marine invertebrates which live on or just under the surface. (Dr. Howard Braham, NMFS)
BELOW — The typical blow which the gray emits from its blowhole is short and widely dispersed. (Cliff Hyatt)
BOTTOM — Barnacles usually grow on the body of a gray whale. (Frank Gardner)

79

more successful quest." According to Dr. Raymond M. Gilmore of the Natural History Museum at San Diego, California, the presence of two males could be a result of a lack of interest in sex by about half the mature females which have newborn calves.

A sexually mature female seems to have one calf every other year. She mates in winter, gives birth in 12 to 13 months, nurses and then weans the calf 6 to 7 months later in the north before migrating south.

In January 1975 scientists Ron Storro-Patterson and John Kipping of the University of California at Berkeley, reported seeing a gray whale give birth off Baja California. "A large gray whale cow made a slow, 360-degree roll close to our drifting boat. As her ventral surface came into view, the rostrum of the calf in the process of being born was seen protruding from her vagina. Seconds later, the calf was on the surface . . . taking its first three breaths unassisted; the cow then lifted the calf clear of the water. The breathing and swimming of the calf were first uncoordinated and labored. . . . After 1½ hours it made a steady swim against a strong current, possibly assisted by its mother."

Studies conducted on gray whales in Alaska since 1975 by Dr. Howard W. Braham, of the Marine Mammal Division, National Marine Fisheries Service, reveal that gray whales remain close to shore throughout their entire migration from Mexico to the Bering Sea. According to Braham, they remain along the shore during their migration to feed. Once in the northern Bering Sea and Arctic Ocean, grays spread out and feed throughout the summer. The fall migration pattern seems to be similar but in the opposite direction. Gray whales enter and leave the Bering Sea through Unimak Pass in the eastern Aleutians.

Gray whales of the Korean herd were taken by the Japanese with nets in the 17th century and members of the California herd were pursued by Indians off the coast of Washington's Olympic Peninsula. But grays were not really threatened until 1852 when the migration of the California herd to nearly landlocked Mexican lagoons was detected by enterprising whalers who killed them by the hundreds. Hunting pressure was relieved just before the turn of the century when a decline in the demand for whale products and a decrease in the number of available animals made whaling uneconomical. But in 1924 factory ships again began hunting gray whales.

In 1937 all grays received some protection under an international treaty, although Japanese and Soviet factory ships continued to pursue them in arctic waters. The numbers, estimated at about 15,000 in the eastern Pacific in 1850, had declined to an estimated 4,400 in 1875. Thirty years ago a complete ban was finally established to protect them. They have made a substantial comeback and current populations are estimated to be between 10,000 and 15,000. □

A gray whale plays in the waters of Scammon's Lagoon, a favorite breeding ground for this species, off Baja California. (Will Anderson)

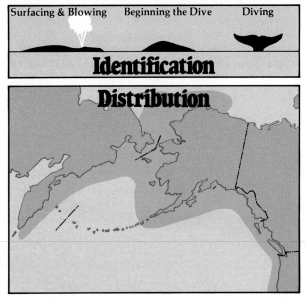

Surfacing & Blowing   Beginning the Dive   Diving

Identification

Distribution

A gray whale cow and calf. A mother will reportedly nurse her offspring for 6 or 7 months. (Frank Gardner)

The waters of Stephens Passage, an 80-mile-long channel from Portland Island to Frederick Sound south of Juneau, in Southeastern Alaska, drip from the flukes of a humpback whale. (Lou Barr)

Humpback

Megaptera novaeangliae

The humpback is a rorqual whale which can be distinguished from other rorquals by its wider and less numerous ventral gooves. It is a cosmopolitan species found in all oceans. In the eastern Pacific humpbacks are distributed from the southeast Bering sea, the Aleutians, Prince William Sound, Glacier Bay and throughout the waterways of Southeastern Alaska in summer. Their winter range shifts south at least as far as Banderas Bay in mainland Mexico, the tip of Baja California and the Hawaiian Islands. Humpbacks are known to migrate, spending the spring, summer and fall months in northern waters where they remain

longer than most whales. In the winter most members of this species head for warmer waters. There may be resident humpback populations in Southeastern Alaska and studies are being conducted to chart the movement of these whales. (See the article by Charles and Virginia Jurasz on humpbacks in Southeastern beginning on page 116.)

Humpbacks feed on krill

and a variety of fish including anchovies, sardines, capelin and herring. In summer feeding grounds they often blow

nets of bubbles to surround and bewilder their prey, then swim through the center of the air ring, jaws open, to scoop up their meal. Prince William Sound is an important summer feeding area for this species.

At a distance humpbacks may be confused with other baleen whales, such as the blue, fin or sei, but at close view misidentification is unlikely. There is a distinct hump in front of the

Of the large whales with a dorsal fin, the humpback is the only species which regularly raises its flukes before diving.

83

ABOVE — The hump in front of the dorsal fin and the irregular shape of the dorsal fin are keys to the identification of a humpback. This animal was photographed in Glacier Bay in Southeastern Alaska. (Jim Hauck)

RIGHT — A humpback displays the ventral surface of its flukes during a dive near Knight Island in Prince William Sound. Scientists have identified individual animals by the white areas which appear on the underside, and sometimes the topside, of the humpback's flukes. (John Hall)

84

Humpbacks are among the more active breachers of the larger whales. And they can be readily identified by their huge flippers, ventral grooves and the bumps on their rostrum. (K. C. Balcomb)

dorsal fin on the back of most humpbacks. Their scalloped, winglike flippers are the largest of any species and reach lengths of from one-fifth to one-third of their 45-foot body length, and are covered on the leading edge with wartlike bumps. Warts are also found on the head, and each sprouts a sensitive whiskerlike vibrissa.

The humpback is basically black with a white area of varying size on its throat; its flippers are all white beneath, usually partially white above; its flukes vary from all white to all black beneath and are usually all black above. This species is unusually susceptible to parasites, especially acorn and stalked barnacles and a small, six-legged marine crustacean which is surprisingly hard to pull from its host. Up to half a ton of barnacles may be attached to a single humpback.

Humpbacks swim at an average of two to five miles an hour and can accelerate to nine or ten miles an hour in flight. This species of whale is the most acrobatic, and often heaves its giant body out of the water in magnificent leaps and turns. Humpbacks are also powerful swimmers. Records show that in 1895 an old bull, harpooned in Henderson Bay near Puget Sound in Washington State, towed a small boat of a whaling party for "five long days and nights" before finally being killed.

On the northern migration humpbacks usually swim in pods of two to five animals with newly pregnant females and immature young leading mature males and other females to the feeding grounds.

According to Allen Wolman, Marine Mammal Division, National Marine Fisheries Service, humpback courtship consists in part of one animal stroking its partner with its entire body and flippers as it glides past. They also give each other playful flipper slaps.

Because the humpback is unusually rich in oil and a slow swimmer, it has long been the target of coastal whalers. There is disagreement over the number of humpbacks before commercial whaling. They did not receive protection until 1965, however, and their current population is thought to be about 7,000 or less. Since they inhabit shallow waters often near population centers, humpbacks are particularly susceptible to the effects of man. Vessel traffic in Southeastern Alaska is one activity that may affect the future of humpback populations in that area. □

HUMPBACK SANCTUARY

A number of organizations interested in the future of marine mammals are working toward the establishment of a sanctuary for these animals off the coast of Hawaii. For details on this project, please contact the Office of Coastal Zone Management, National Marine Sanctuaries Program, 3300 Whitehaven Street N.W., Washington, D.C. 20235, and the Marine Mammal Commission, 1625 Eye Street N.W., Washington, D.C. 20006.

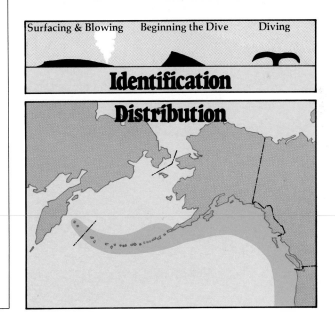

Surfacing & Blowing   Beginning the Dive   Diving

Identification
Distribution

A humpback blowing. The head in front of the blowhole is flattened and dotted with wartlike bumps. (Aaron Avellar)

Giant Bottlenose

Berardius bairdi

The giant bottlenose whale, also known as Baird's beaked whale, is a toothed cetacean second in size only to the sperm whale. This species is only found in the North Pacific and has been reported from Saint Matthew Island in the Bering Sea to 29° north, about the latitude of the northern half of Baja California. In all seasons giant bottlenose whales appear to be present off central California.

Giant bottlenose whales feed primarily on squid, although they reportedly also eat octopus, rockfish and herring. Even though they are toothed whales, giant bottlenose whales have only two pair of teeth (which emerge above the gums only in adult males) on the lower jaw and none on the upper jaw.

At a distance, this species may be confused with related beaked whales or with the minke whale; however the giant bottlenose generally inhabits waters deeper than those normally frequented by minkes. The bulbous head, color, dorsal fin and dorsal ridge of the giant bottlenose whale are quite distinctive at close range. When surfacing to breathe, the giant bottlenose whale often brings its head out of the water at an angle that clearly shows its beak, which is long like that of a bottlenose dolphin. In the adult male the lower jaw extends well past the tip of the upper jaw.

Giant bottlenose whales are slate gray to army brown, usually with numerous scratches, and their undersides generally have a few white blotches. Males commonly reach 30 to 36 feet in length;

Little is known about the giant bottlenose whale, a deepwater, toothed cetacean, which is second in size only to the sperm whale.

females tend to be slightly larger. The largest reliably measured specimen was 42 feet long.

Giant bottlenose whales are social animals, swimming in pods of up to 20, but they are difficult for whale watchers to approach. Biologists believe this species is deep diving but actually little is known of its habits. The blow of the giant bottlenose whale is low and indistinct.

Members of this species were occasionally taken by whalers off California and they are hunted off Japan. Since funds for whale research are usually allocated for exploited whale species, population figures for nonexploited species, such as the giant bottlenose, are poorly researched and difficult to determine. □

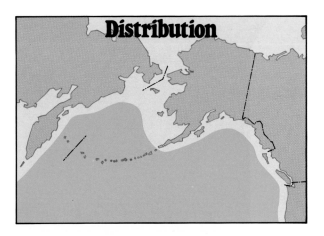

Distribution

A short, triangular-shaped dorsal fin, which protrudes from the last third of the back, is a key to the identification of a giant bottlenose whale. (K. C. Balcomb)

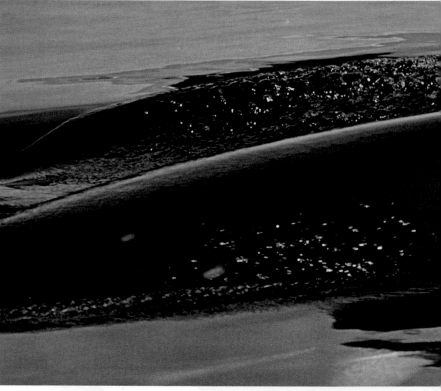

Minkes are the smallest
of the baleen whales
in the Northern
Hemisphere.

ABOVE — A minke exposes its large, sickle-shaped dorsal fin as it surfaces to
breathe near Perry Island in Prince William Sound.
RIGHT — A minke cruises through the waters of Prince William Sound
near Naken Island. The blow of this species is usually low and indistinct.
(Both photos by John Hall)

Minke

Balaenoptera acutorostrata

Minke (prounounced minky) whales are also known as piked whales, little piked whales and lesser rorquals.

This species is widely distributed in many oceans, and is thought to be common in the waters from southern California north to the Bering and Chukchi seas, extending its range into the more northerly waters only in the summer. In winter its range shifts southward. Minkes are believed to be very migratory and are known to favor icy waters to a greater extent than other baleen whales except the bowhead and the gray.

In southern oceans minkes feed almost exclusively on krill, but in the northern oceans they eat primarily mackerel, cod and herring.

The minke is grayish black on its back and white on its stomach, the underside of its tail and flippers. There is also a distinct marking to identify members of this species which come from the northern and southern oceans. Minkes that inhabit the northern waters have a white band across their flippers—a stripe that is usually lacking in animals from southern waters. It is thought that there may be

Up, up and crash. A minke breaches in Prince William Sound and returns to the water with a resounding splash. (Both photos by Donald G. Calkins)

96

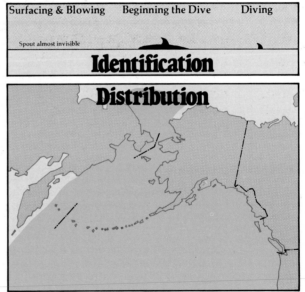

Minkes of the North Pacific and North Atlantic vary slightly in coloration, especially in the degree of white on their bodies. This is a North Atlantic minke photographed off Cape Cod. (Aaron Avellar)

Surfacing & Blowing	Beginning the Dive	Diving
Spout almost invisible		

Identification

Distribution

several stocks of minkes which vary from region to region.

Minkes, the smallest baleen whale in the Northern Hemisphere may reach 33 feet in length. Usually they are smaller, however, and are not as large as their Southern Hemisphere counterparts.

Minkes are among the faster swimmers of the large whales and can move along at 16 to 21 miles an hour. Often they swim alone but are known to concentrate in rich feeding areas in the spring and summer.

Minkes were of little interest to commercial whalers in the past. But because of the richness of their meat and the depletion of other species, minkes are the most heavily harvested baleen whale today.

Before the advent of commercial whaling the minke whale population was said to have reached 360,000; current population figures are difficult to estimate but there are believed to be less than 100,000 in the North Pacific. □

Killer

Orcinus orca

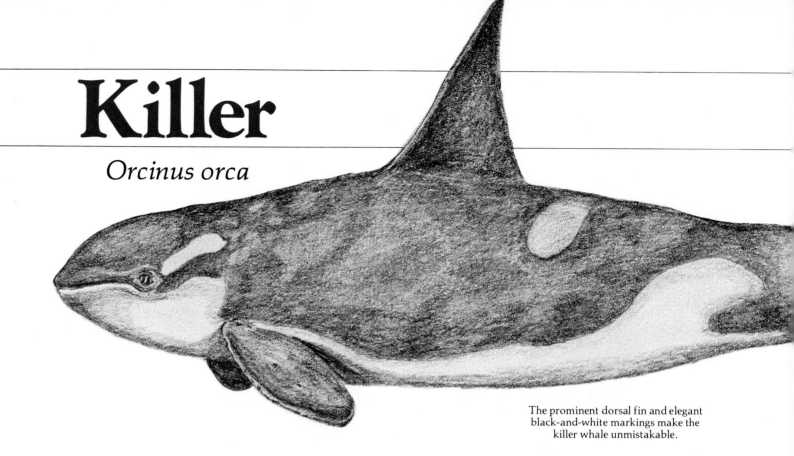

The prominent dorsal fin and elegant black-and-white markings make the killer whale unmistakable.

Killer whales are also known as orcas, or wolves of the sea. They are carnivorous cetaceans that feed on a wide variety of marine animals. The stomach contents of ten killer whales collected in waters from Kodiak Island in the Gulf of Alaska to San Miguel Island off Santa Barbara, California, by Dale Rice, Marine Mammal Division, National Marine Fisheries Service, included the remains of three California sea lions, four Steller sea lions, seven elephant seals, two harbor porpoises, two Dall porpoises, one minke whale, one halibut, two sharks and a squid.

Killers sometimes hunt in pods or teams, appear capable of following complex, cooperative patterns in their attack, and have successfully taken on larger whales including the gray, blue and minke. Eskimos have told of seeing killer whales pursuing bowheads until the larger but slower bowheads retreated under the pack ice. Six orcas killed a minke on the Fairweather Grounds in the Gulf of Alaska on April 29, 1976, as scientists aboard a Na-

ABOVE — A killer whale spy hopping. (K. C. Balcomb)
LEFT — Killer whales washed up on the beach at Hesquiat Harbor near Estevan Point, British Columbia, about 1947. Echolocation, a system of location associated primarily with toothed cetaceans, can occasionally lead animals astray and cause them to become trapped in shallow waters. (Provincial Archives, Victoria, British Columbia)

A killer whale breaching.
Male killers are unlikely to be
confused with any other
cetacean, but females and
immatures could possibly be
confused with false killer
whales. However, the white
markings, broader-shaped
head and larger size will
distinguish a killer whale.
(K. C. Balcomb)

100

The dorsal fin of the adult male killer whale can reach 6 feet in height; that of the female and immature killer is usually much smaller (about 3 feet is common) and more curved. (Graeme Ellis)

tional Oceanic and Atmospheric Administration (NOAA) research vessel watched.

Killer whale attacks on boats are rare and poorly documented and there has been only one unsubstantiated kill of a human—a Mexican fisherman off Baja California in 1977.

Killer whales range from the Beaufort Sea to Antarctica. They are most abundant off the Aleutians and there seem to be resident populations in some areas, such as Puget Sound in Washington State. Scientists also believe that some killer whales migrate, riding cold currents south in winter.

Male killer whales average 23 feet in length and one individual was measured at 31 feet. Females of this species are smaller.

The most unusual feature of the killer whale is its high, triangular to sickle-shaped dorsal fin, which has no muscle but may serve the whale as a keel would a boat. The dorsal fin of old males may reach 6 feet in height; that of females and immatures is much smaller.

Because of this prominent fin, the mature male killer whale is unlikely to be confused with any other species. However, Dall porpoises are often mistaken for young killer whales. From a distance false killer whales might be mistaken for female or immature killers. But these blackfish are smaller, rarely exceeding 18 feet; are more slender than true killer whales; and are all black; whereas orcas have white bellies and flanks and white markings on their heads.

Killer whales have been clocked swimming at a steady 25 knots and in one radio-tracking study some moving

A killer whale swims just below the surface.
Scientists and whale enthusiasts are still
debating whether the killer whale is a threat to
humans. There are few documented cases of
killer whale attacks and these have been
provoked, but killer whales are certainly
capable of doing great harm and should be
treated with respect. (K. C. Balcomb)

Surfacing & Blowing	Beginning the Dive	Diving
	Male Female	

Identification

Distribution

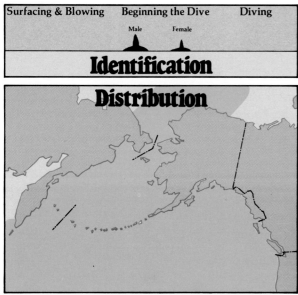

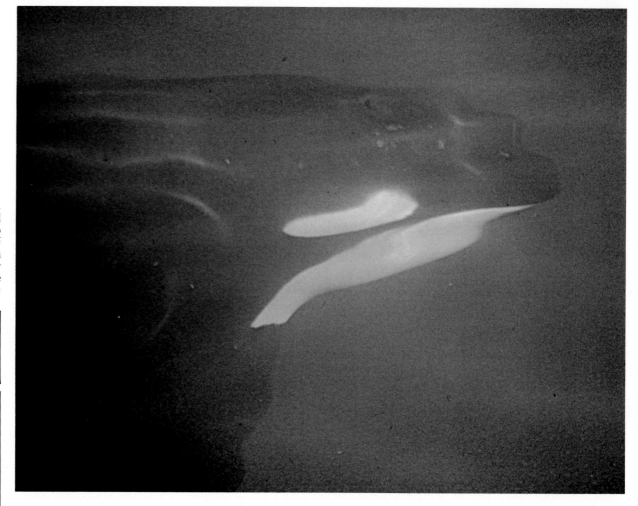

102

When chased by killer whales, sea lions will take shelter against whatever they can, in this case a boat. In the top photo, a killer whale watches the sea lion herd which is huddled off the bow of a Japanese stern trawler. In the photo above, the sea lions swim frantically off the bow of the ship, with killer whales in the foreground. The sea lions are porpoising and scared. (Mil Zahn, NMFS)

groups averaged 75 miles a day. Speeds that would allow a pod of killer whales to move 75 miles a day may not be normal, however, but a response to the tracking vessel.

Early whalers hunting baleen whales off New South Wales, Australia, were at first alarmed to discover that killer whales accompanied the larger whales. The hunters, unable to drive off the orcas, then discovered that the killers seemed to be after only the lips and tongues of the big baleens and otherwise did not disturb the carcasses. In the seasons that followed, a strange cooperation developed between the orcas and the hunters. The killer whales, which often were the first to spot the baleen whales at sea, would alert the whalers on shore and, like harbor pilots, convey the boatman to within harpoon range, then stand by for the kill. The killer whales came to know the schedule of the whalers and showed up to greet them regularly.

Killers are thought to be highly intelligent and to possess all the human senses except smell. To sleep, killer whales take catnaps on the surface. And because they are used to hunting, captive killer whales generally refuse dead food at first. Namu, one of the first killer whales to be taken alive, weighed in at 7,520 pounds and at first refused everything but salmon—200 pounds a day.

In courtship the male killer whale ac-tively seeks to attract the apparently indifferent female, dancing around her in a circle of marvelous leaps, and beating the water to a froth right under her nose. If he is successful, the female will allow him to caress her with his flippers and finally roll on her side in which position mating may take place. Afterwards, the animals sometimes rest, motionless on the water's surface.

At birth a baby killer whale is about 40% of the length of its mother, fully formed and ready to perform the usual swimming feats soon after it takes its first breath. The mother nurses her young from one of her two breasts, on the surface, rolling on her side and ejecting milk by muscular contraction into the baby's mouth. Squirting the milk, which contains six times as much protein as human milk, into the baby's mouth allows the newborn to breathe while feeding. Killer whales have a life expectancy of 30 to 40 years.

Except in Japan and Norway, killer whales were seldom sought by commercial whalers and, although the Quillayute and Makah Indians of Washington State are said to have hunted them, few other Native people cared to try because they believed that the hunted killer whale would seek revenge. For this reason and because the killer whale has no natural enemy, the populations of this species appear to be healthy and subject only to nature's balance of food availability. □

Beluga

Delphinapterus leucas

Belugas are called "canaries of the sea" because of their noisy chatter and "white whales" because of their color. The word beluga is Russian for sturgeon; *Belukha* is the Russian word for the beluga whale.

This small, toothed whale prefers icy waters but is also found as far south as Cook Inlet and Yakutat Bay on the west coast of North America and as far south as the Gulf of St. Lawrence on the east coast. The species has been spotted swimming 1,240 miles up the Amur River in Asia, and 600 miles inland in the Yukon River. It has also been seen in Lake Iliamna, on the Alaska Peninsula.

Belugas are closely related to the tusked narwhal and the young of the two species are difficult to tell apart. Otherwise, belugas cannot easily be mistaken for any other species because of their unusual white color. Young belugas are bluish gray but change to pure white on reaching sexual maturity which takes 4 to 5 years. At full growth belugas are 15 to 16 feet long.

The beluga has no dorsal fin. This allows the animal to move easily under the ice and, indeed, it can sometimes be spotted sleeping under clear, newly formed ice. Belugas navigate by echolocation and, according to Stephen Leatherwood, NOSC, they have the most sophisticated biosonar yet studied.

Belugas are masters of echolocation and seem capable of moving comfortably through the ice-clogged waterways of their frigid arctic habitat.

LEFT — A pod of beluga whales. The distinctive white coloring of these small toothed whales makes them easy to identify. (Leslie Nakashima, reprinted from *ALASKA GEOGRAPHIC*®)

105

RIGHT — Belugas swim through an ice lead north of Point Barrow, Alaska. (Jack W. Lentfer)
BELOW — Belugas are toothed whales which feed on fish, such as cod and capelin, on squid and on an assortment of marine crustaceans found near the ocean floor. (W. J. Houck)

106

Belugas are generally slow swimmers, usually moving less than 5 or 6 miles an hour but they can reach speeds of 12 miles an hour. Even so, they are still an easy target for their enemy, the killer whale, which can sprint at 30 miles an hour or more.

White whales are highly social, often traveling in pods of several hundred, and they migrate with the bowheads in the spring. They are also curious about humans and often will approach small boats and people on ice floes, sometimes inspecting them carefully.

Belugas eat fish, squid and marine invertebrates. Their usual method of feeding is to grip their prey with their teeth and swallow it whole.

About the turn of the century a small but highly profitable industry was founded to hunt the beluga for its skin, which is marketed under the name "porpoise hide" and still commands a good price as glove leather. The oil from the beluga is extremely high grade and its muktuk (blubber) is regarded as a delicacy both by some Eskimos and Japanese.

Despite the fact that they are commercially valuable and disliked by some salmon fishermen because they feed on salmon fry, stocks of beluga whales seem to be holding up well. Resident populations in Cook Inlet are currently estimated at from 300 to 400 animals; in Bristol Bay at between 1,000 and 1,500; and populations in Alaskan waters to the north may number 8,000.

Summer and fall populations in the Canadian Arctic which appear to come from Alaskan waters are thought to be between 4,000 and 6,000 but the migration patterns of these animals are not yet clear and there may be double counting. ☐

Belugas seem to prefer a shallow water environment and can be found in the estuarine areas along Alaska's coast. Partially because of their smaller size, belugas seem to have adapted well to captivity. (W. J. Houck)

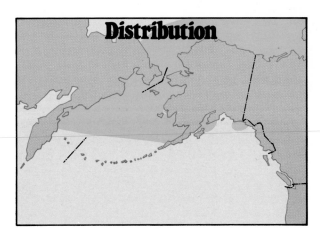

Distribution

Narwhal

Monodon monoceros
By Randall R. Reeves

Normally only male narwhals sport the single tusk, which gives these animals their nickname of sea unicorn.

Imagine the puzzled look on Conrad Killingivuk's face in late October 1971 when he found a unicorn on the sandspit north of the village of Point Hope. The unicorn was actually a young male narwhal with a spiraled tusk, about a yard long, jutting from the left side of its upper jaw.

Only three species of whales are fulltime residents of arctic waters, and the narwhal is one of them. Alaskans are more familiar with the other two: the bowhead and the beluga. The narwhal is very rarely encountered in Alaska.

Charles Brower reportedly saw only two of them during his 40 years at Point Barrow around the turn of the century. In fact, he claimed that "the narwhal [was] so seldom seen in northern Alaska waters that the local Eskimos have no name for it." F. H. Fay, a marine mammalogist at the University of Alaska, Fairbanks, says that the Saint Lawrence Islanders actually do have a name for it — *bousuck-tugutalik*, or "beluga with tusk." Records of "extralimital" narwhals should be of particular interest to Alaskans, for whom the sight of this almost-mythical creature is a novel possibility.

In the summer of 1928 an Eskimo acquired the skull of a male narwhal with a 4½-foot-long tusk from near Cape Halkett, Harrison Bay, at the mouth of the Colville River on the Beaufort Sea coast. On September 1, 1929, Pete Savolik of Barrow found the carcass of a narwhal on a beach near Atigaru Point, also on the Beaufort Sea. Almost 30 years later (in August 1957), George Moto, an Eskimo from Candle, chanced upon another beached narwhal at Kiwalik Lagoon, 4 miles north-east of Candle. In addition to a 3-foot-long tusk, this 13½-foot whale had what appeared to be the 5-inch tip of another narwhal's tusk embedded in the left upper jaw. As far as I know, this is the only report of such a circumstance, and it suggests that the tusk may be used for fighting among males.

Earlier that year, in April, a live narwhal had become stranded in the surf at the mouth of the Caribou River in Nelson Lagoon on the Alaska Peninsula. It was thrashing violently in a few inches of water, and gulls and bald eagles had begun to peck at its flesh. Mercifully, a local resident shot it. The 14-foot carcass (and its 7-foot tusk) washed away, unfortunately, before it could be recovered for scientific study. This is the only recorded instance of the species' occurrence on the Alaska coast south of the Bering Strait.

There are also more recent reports, including one of a narwhal said to have been seen with a pod of belugas west of Barrow in May 1976, and one found dead at Pingu Bluff (north of Barrow) in the fall of 1973. The latter reportedly possessed a 20-inch tusk that, like Conrad Killingivuk's, was traded to a nonresident before it could be used to verify the record.

Narwhal tusks have been found on Saint Lawrence Island and at Wainwright, and a report exists of a harpoon foreshaft receiver made of narwhal ivory being purchased at

At Kakiak Point on the west shore of Admiralty Inlet in the Canadian Arctic, an Eskimo family prepares to haul a large bull narwhal ashore. Its 6-foot tusk should bring about $300 to the hunter. (Randall R. Reeves)

109

A beached male narwhal. A
narwhal is dark bluish to
brownish and is often spotted
which makes it easy to
distinguish from the only
other medium-sized cetacean
which inhabits its
environment, the all white
beluga. (Fred Bruemmer)

Kotzebue in the 1930's. It is likely that some narwhal ivory has found its way to Alaska through trade with Eskimos of eastern Canada or possibly Siberia. However, the occasional records of specimens washing ashore or being killed off Alaska indicate that narwhals do come here on their own accord, straying far beyond their normal range. It is impossible to guess where these strays originated. Russian sources indicate that narwhals are present in the Chukchi Sea, and they are certainly common in the eastern Arctic of Canada as far west as Cornwallis Island. But whether the animals seen off Alaska are eastbound, westbound or part of a small, local stock is impossible to tell.

During the late 19th century the Scandinavian explorer Baron N.A.E. Nordenskjold retold a story he had heard while visiting Bering Island in the southwestern Bering Sea: in 1854 local residents had observed a Steller sea cow. Nordenskjold's report sent a shudder of excitement through the international zoological community, because this huge marine herbivore had been presumed extinct since at least 1768. Leonard Stejneger, the biographer of the sea cow's namesake, Georg W. Steller, hurried to the scene, where he personally reinterviewed Nordenskjold's informants. This visit left Stejneger with little doubt that the Natives had seen "an animal unknown to them"; but his conclusion about its identity and the reasoning behind it were considerably more plausible than Nordenskjold's. The 14- to 18-foot-long creature had been shaped like a whale and had behaved like a whale; it had had no fin on its back and its coloration was "light brownish white, with round or oblong dark spots." Stejneger asserted that "this description exactly fits the female narwhal."

Stories like that told by Nordenskjold don't die easily, however. In 1963 three Russian scientists reported that whalers working off the coast of Cape Navarin (west and somewhat south of Saint Lawrence Island) in July 1962 had seen a Steller sea cow. Their story has been discredited, however, partly on the basis of the locality of the sighting (Steller sea cows supposedly were confined to the vicinity of the Commander Islands in the southern Bering Sea at the time of their discovery in 1741-42) and partly because the description given by the whalers sounded as much like a female narwhal as like a Steller sea cow. Nevertheless, there are those who cling to the belief that somewhere out there a sea cow (or two) survives, and that one day its hiding place will be revealed.

The narwhal resembles the beluga in body size and shape. Large males have been measured at 16 feet in length and found to weigh nearly 2 tons. The narwhal has a blunt, rounded head and only the slightest hint of a beak. Like the bowhead and beluga, it has no dorsal fin — just a kind of ridge along its spine where the fin would be expected in another species. The flippers are small and softly rounded, while the tail flukes are relatively large, delicately curved and fan shaped. Newborn nar-

A close-up of the face of a young male narwhal. Note how white mottling has begun to appear. Also the tusk, which in this case was only about a foot long, can be seen to protrude from the left side of the upper jaw. (Mich Zeman, courtesy of Randall R. Reeves, reprinted from *ALASKA* ® magazine)

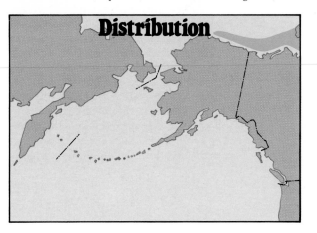

Distribution

A wary narwhal mother lifts her infant clear of the water for a quick breath. This behavior is not uncommon among cetaceans, particularly when the calf is very young and is being disturbed by a boat. (Randall R. Reeves)

whals (about 5 feet in length) are gray. Soon afterward, probably by the end of their first year, they become uniformly black. As they grow older, white mottling appears on the belly, gradually spreading up the flanks and in some cases onto the dorsal surface. It is probably from the paleness of older animals that the species' common name was derived; *nar* means "corpse" in Old Norse.

The function of the male narwhal's tusk is open to question. Some have judged it to be an ice piercer; others have regarded it as a kind of plow for stirring up prey on the ocean bottom. It appears to be a lethal enough weapon, for fencing with or ramming an opponent. One ingenious scientist speculated that it might be a very useful projector or director of sound waves. Today the conventional wisdom seems to be that this curious implement is little more than an extravagant adornment to assist the male in wooing females for mating. Whatever its purpose, it can hardly be essential to survival, for females manage fine without one.

One of nature's more tragic quirks is the phenomenon known as *savssat* (pronounced sset). It happens to both narwhals and belugas when groups of either species are trapped in enclosed waters by sudden ice formation. Once the animals are sealed off from the open sea, the area in which they can maneuver for breath becomes more and more constricted. Sometimes several hundred whales are crowded into a small breathing hole, and they become

easy targets for hunters. In the severe winter of 1914-15, two *savssats* were discovered by Eskimos in Disko Bay, West Greenland. The harvest at these two sites amounted to more than 1,000 narwhals, according to M. P. Porsild, a Danish scientist who was there.

Narwhals have no teeth, as we commonly think of them, only the long spike that protrudes from the male's upper jaw and one mature but unerupted tooth (two in females) embedded in the upper jawbone. On very rare occasions, two-tusked narwhals have been caught or seen; oddly enough, these have often been females. Seven- or eight-foot-long tusks are not uncommon for old bulls, and these ivory appendages can weigh up to 20 pounds. Since the wholesale value of raw ivory now exceeds $30 a pound, there is a real incentive for hunting narwhals in areas where they are abundant.

The narwhal is confined primarily to deep canyons and fjords of the northern North Atlantic, particularly in the eastern Canadian archipelago, Baffin Bay and the Greenland Sea. What attracts narwhals to deep water is not clear. Perhaps it has something to do with their diet, which is said to consist in large part of squid and pelagic fish. Narwhals seldom stray far from pack ice, and they apparently can give birth successfully in the frigid Arctic Basin.

The natural history of the narwhal is not very well understood. During the last several years the Canadian government has become concerned about the

species' future and has sponsored a modest research program, centered on the north coast of Baffin Island, where the Eskimos of Pond Inlet and Arctic Bay energetically hunt the narwhal. From catch statistics and samples of whales taken, Keith Hay and David Sergeant of the Arctic Biological Station in Quebec have developed much new insight on such things as the rate of calf production, age at sexual maturity, and the impact of hunting on the whale population.

In the summer of 1975 I went to Arctic Bay, where I met two technicians from the Arctic Biological Station. They had been posted there to observe the hunt, photograph and measure killed narwhals and collect biological specimens. In addition to the 15 or 20 animals that we examined together, we saw hundreds more in ice-infested Admiralty Inlet during July and August.

Counting whales even under ideal conditions is difficult, and narwhals who spend most of their lives well north of the Arctic Circle present an almost impossible task. Nevertheless, a promising method was tried recently in Canada. Two biologists were stationed on a clifftop overlooking the southern shore of Lancaster Sound. They spent 6 weeks at Cape Hay in the summer of 1976, patiently enumerating the narwhals swimming by beneath them. Since virtually all the animals passing Cape Hay at this season are heading west, it was felt that the chances of double counting were quite low. Their total of 6,145 narwhals seen is almost

A female narwhal with her recently born calf glide through a shallow stretch of Admiralty Inlet in the Canadian Arctic. (Randall R. Reeves, reprinted from *ALASKA*® magazine)

113

Three young narwhals (note the absence of white mottling) were killed just beyond the ice floes. Here they are being towed ashore, where they will be flensed quickly, before the rising tide reclaims their carcasses. None were tusked, but the muktuk from these three animals will be utilized. (Randall R. Reeves)

identical to an estimate made by an ornithologist who was studying murres at Cape Hay 19 years earlier. Since visibility was poor during part of the period in which the westward migration seemed to be reaching a peak, the observers felt that perhaps 8,000 to 10,000 animals actually passed Cape Hay in 1976. Other biologists, sponsored by a Canadian oil concern, were trying to count narwhals from the air during the same summer. Since their range of observation extended across the entire breadth of Lancaster Sound, they were able to document the presence of many narwhals beyond the sight of the shore-based team. Consequently, an alternative estimate of as many as 20,000 to 30,000 narwhals in the region was developed.

Obviously, the narwhal population in Lancaster Sound is large, and it may be capable of withstanding a sizable Native harvest. The Eskimos of Arctic Bay and Pond Inlet make a substantial catch, especially during years when ice conditions allow easy access to the floe edge in early summer. I was told that during breakup in 1974, Arctic Bay hunters brought home more than 100 tusks from a 3-day stint on the ice. The following summer only about 10 tusks were secured before the ice became unsafe.

During the open-water season (usually part of July, all of August and part of September) entire families leave the settlement and camp along the shores of Admiralty Inlet. There they pursue narwhals and seals and live off the land, very much as their ancestors did centuries ago. The monetary value of ivory tusks and sealskins encourages hunting. While hunters hunt selectively for tusked narwhals, they often must settle for the more accessible females and young animals without tusks, which they kill for food alone (muktuk — whale skin — and seal meat are still important elements in the local diet). In 1976 the Canadian government established annual quotas allocated on a settlement-by-settlement basis. If enforced, these measures should constitute an adequate guarantee for a thriving narwhal herd.

Alaska, of course, is not likely ever to have a narwhal conservation problem, since too few of these exotic whales visit its coastal waters to support any significant hunting activity. However, it is to be hoped that those who do find their way here will not be harmed. □

Editor's note: *Randall R. Reeves is a research collaborator at the Smithsonian Institution and works with the National Fish and Wildlife Laboratory and the Marine Mammal Commission. His special interest is arctic marine mammals. This article appeared in a slightly different form in the September 1978 issue of ALASKA®.*

A humpback breaches near Columbia Glacier in Prince William Sound. Rick Latta was aboard the ferry *Bartlett* and took this photo while the ferry circled the whale to observe its behavior.

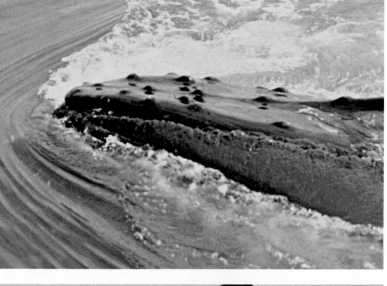

CLOCKWISE FROM RIGHT — Looking into the open mouth of a feeding humpback; the lower jaw is on top. Humpbacks often feed upside down. / The snout of a humpback. Note the bumps which are especially characteristic of this species. (Both photos by Bruce Wellman, courtesy of Charles Jurasz) / A humpback pectoral fin. These huge fins rotate forward in a clearing-the-table-style sweep when the animal is feeding. / The back and dorsal fin of a humpback. (Both photos by Charles Jurasz)

By *CHARLES and VIRGINIA JURASZ*

Humpback Whales in Southeastern Alaska

The humpback whale is a coast-loving species that feeds close to shore in bays and fjords. This accessibility to man has led to its destruction over a recorded span of 20 years. Formerly, there were many humpbacks in the eastern Aleutian and western Alaska Peninsula waters; estimates ranged from 4,000 to 6,000 humpbacks in Alaska waters alone. In 1975, a census was conducted by vessel and aircraft in Southeastern Alaska and 60 humpbacks were counted throughout the inside passages and along the outer coast. Although all hunting of the humpbacks ceased in 1966, by 1970 the humpback was declared an endangered species.

The average adult humpback is 40 to 50 feet in length, and the female is usually the larger. For every foot in length, a humpback weighs about 1,500 pounds. A 45-foot humpback could weigh 35 tons.

The most distinctive feature of the humpback is its pectoral fins, which appear as arms of 12 to 13 feet in length. The pectoral flippers, scalloped on the leading edge, are supple enough to arch gracefully either across the stomach or across the back. These fins can lie along the body in a kind of hands-at-the-side position and yet articulate fully forward in a clearing-the-table-style sweep while in feeding maneuvers. At such times the

ABOVE — Small by comparison, a boatman watches the flukes of a humpback sink beneath the surface. (Bruce Wellman, courtesy of Charles Jurasz)

117

CLOCKWISE FROM RIGHT — Pleats in the throat of a humpback which is swimming on its side and feeding. / Coloration on the flukes is used to identify individuals in the humpback population in Southeastern. The large amount of white on the underside of the flukes identifies this animal as Garfunkel. / A look in the mouth of a feeding humpback shows the inside of the upper jaw and the baleen plates. / In this view of the feeding humpback on the left, the top of the upper jaw is visible. The dorsal fin of a second humpback swimming alongside is also shown. (All photos by Bruce Wellman, courtesy of Charles Jurasz)

118

whales seem to be veritably climbing through the feed mouth first.

Generally, the color of the humpback is black above and white or gray below, but each humpback's coloration seems to be different. As a result, the patterns of white and black on the undersides of the tail and the pectoral fins and on the sides of the dorsal fin can be used to identify the whale just as facial characteristics are used to identify a person. Color patterns vary with different geographic areas. The humpback whales of Southeastern Alaska are predominantly black with very little white, occasionally a whale with an all white tail on the underside is seen. Stocks in Hawaii and the West Indies seem to have much more white on the undersides of their tails and flippers. Attempts are being made to identify individual whales by their natural markings in order to piece together the whale's migration patterns and to try to establish a more accurate worldwide census of the humpback.

In Southeastern Alaska, photographs of tail patterns and dorsal fin characteristics have been employed in censusing since 1968 and indications are that these colorations last at least three years, if not a lifetime. Four whales, which have been returning to the same area of Glacier Bay National Monument to feed for the past three years, have been identified by their natural markings, which have not changed during this three-year period. [**Editor's note:** *Anyone who has clearly photographed a fluke pattern—underside of the tail—of a humpback may send the photo to the Juraszes, P.O. Box 93, Auke Bay, Alaska 99821, with information as to where and when taken. Through the identification of these whales via natural markings, it can be determined if whales are returning to or spending a large portion of their lives in Alaska waters.*]

Observation of live whales and dissection of carcasses have led to some intriguing facts about humpbacks. On the face of each humpback whale are tubercles, or bumps, on the snout, chin and lips. Each tubercle contains a single hair. There is considerable variation between the number of tubercles on each whale. A count of tubercles on 62 whales was made during the time of the whaling fleets, and the number varied from 9 to 27 on different whales.

A baleen whale, the humpback whale uses baleen plates, its mouth opening, tongue, and ventral grooves, to feed. The baleen plates are very coarse and have a composition similar to that of human fingernails. The inside edges of the plates end in coarse bristles that are similar in appearance to matted goat hair. The color of the plates varies from gray to almost black and the bristles from white to grayish white. The number of plates in an adult humpback's mouth varies from 600 to 800 in the whole mouth, or 300 to 400 on one side. The roof of a whale's mouth is empty of plates and gives the appearance of having been parted down the middle.

The ventral grooves or pleats in the chin of the humpback extend from the lips, or mandible, two-thirds of the way down the body. (Using the human body for comparison, the pleats would run from the lips to the knees.) The pleated throat expands to allow the humpback to engulf huge quantities of water and feed (krill). When the mouth is shut, the feed is contained by the matted inner surface of the baleen and the water is expelled through this matting and the spaces between the plates. The body pleats are much farther apart on the humpback than on other baleen whales, and there are only about 24 pleats between pectoral flippers.

A humpback whale can open its mouth 90 degrees, and when its mouth is agape and its pleated throat is distended, the story of Jonah is suddenly very believable.

The humpback whale's most impressive activity in the waters of Southeastern Alaska is feeding, and Southeastern is the only place where feeding humpbacks can be consistently observed and where the feed can be determined by direct observation. The calm inland waters, although usually too full of planktonic life to allow significant underwater visibility, do allow observation of feed in a humpback's mouth and at the water's surface, just prior to the whale's feeding lunge.

This humpback, White Eyes, is recognized by the small patches of white sprinkled on the tips of its fluke. (Bruce Wellman, courtesy of Charles Jurasz)

TOP — A humpback thrusts its bulk out of the water in a half-body breach, giving the animal a profile similar to that of an alligator.
ABOVE — Water drips from the flukes of a humpback after the animal completes a feeding lunge. (Both photos by Charles Jurasz)

120

The humpback is far-ranging and can therefore examine areas for feed potential with relative ease. Although its body is rather stubby appearing, the humpback has little difficulty maintaining a four-knot headway.

Our observation technique is simply a matter of allowing the whales to define the value of an area by their behavior. Collectively the hour-by-hour shifts in their behavior define the value of the place in which the activity occurs. Several areas in Southeastern have thus been defined as having very discrete value for the whales at different times of the year. The greatest seasonal aggregation of humpbacks numbers about 40 in midsummer. These whales disperse from Tracy Arm to Point Gardner to Point Whitney, an area generally described as Frederick Sound, 70 miles south of Juneau along Stephens Passage. This group of whales, the largest stable group in any one place in Southeastern, uses the sound as a primary feeding area and focuses its efforts on euphausiids, a tiny shrimplike animal sometimes called krill. In late July and early August, these waters support a bloom of krill so rich that in the past two years the beaches have been colored light pink when the retreating tide left millions of krill to perish.

A second area frequented by approximately 20 humpbacks during the summer is Glacier Bay. Although closer to the open sea than Frederick Sound, this area has such a tremendous quantity of glacial meltwater that the salinity in many areas of the bay is only 50% —half that of normal sea water. Glacier Bay does support a rich bloom of krill in late July and early August and prior to that it seems that the whales using the bay as early as June feed quite well on at least two of the several species of shrimp which flourish in the silt-rich shelves at the glaciers' face.

Other areas in Southeastern Alaska once supported numerous whales from summer to late fall on the once-ubiquitous herring found in Lynn Canal, Auke Bay and Seymour Canal. But the numbers of these fine little fish have diminished, and the whales are seen less frequently in these areas.

For all its beauty, the humpback whale becomes no more than a streamlined Second World War landing craft at mealtime with a hinge-action maw setting out to engulf all it can. When the feed is dense, the humpback whale dives below the feed and then comes lunging through with its mouth open. Appropriately, this method is called lunge feeding. During this feeding, the movement of the flipper forward along the mouth might be related to maneuvering the animal's 40-ton bulk so close to the surface. But it is also possible that the lighter color on the inside, or underside, of the whale's flipper may assist in chasing the feed into the concentrated mass seen at the surface as the whale lunges through it.

This feeding maneuver, a headlong plunge into the midst, is at first glance an awkward routine. It appears to consist of a luxurious, rolling, snapping bite. There is a shallow dive, the whale circles back on its side, quickly kicks its massive flukes and gulps 150 gallons of food, water and air. This typical feeding behavior may go on for three hours or longer. Hopefully, as these whales become better understood they, too, will demonstrate that the employment of different feeding mechanisms in various parts of their range is a matter of energy efficiency.

When food is available en masse, the technique may be sloppy so long as it remains effective, but at the point at which lunge feeding costs more energy than it yields in food, the behavior changes. As the food source is depleted, the whales are forced to corral, or at least do a bit of herding to make the strong swimming gyrations worthwhile.

One of the most exciting herding techniques is that of bubblenet feeding which was first alluded to in a 1929 French manuscript by a Norwegian named Ingebrigtsen who had been whaling in the Arctic Ocean. The technique was not seen again or recorded anywhere in the world until we observed it in Southeastern Alaska in 1968.

In bubblenet feeding, the whale locates a body of feed, dives below the feed, and discharges a line of bubbles from its blowhole while swimming in a broad

RIGHT — As impressive in grace as intelligence, two humpback whales have blown an underwater ring of bubbles around a school of herring, containing and condensing them. Having completed the bubblenet, the pair share the prized fishes. The second humpback surfaced within the ring moments after this photo was taken. (Robert E. Johnson)

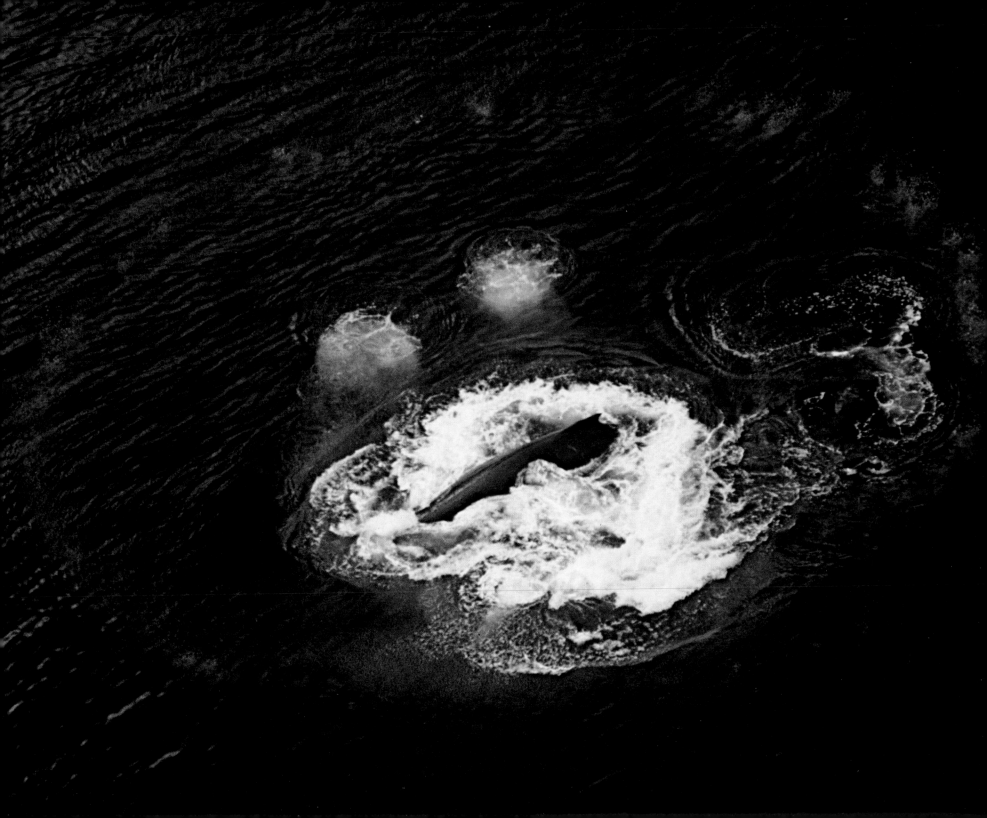

CLOCKWISE FROM RIGHT — Bubbles rise
to the surface as a humpback beneath
the surface closes its mouth
underwater while bubblenet
feeding. / A resting calf exhaling. / A
resting adult humpback. (All photos
by Charles Jurasz)

122

arc, which has both vertical and horizontal components. The whale, outswimming the feed, deploys the bubbles, while sweeping both ahead of the feed and toward the surface. The feed is blocked from below by the whale's body, blocked laterally by the rising bubbles and, ultimately, blocked above by the surface. The feed is thus contained and since it is driven to the surface, it is condensed, by the same action. When the feed is herring, there is a mad frenzy of fish visibly boiling to the water's surface only within the confines of the blown net. If the feed is euphausiids, a blush or a roughing of the water's surface occurs within the ring as the tiny shrimplike feed leap an inch or so into the air. At the point at which the ring or spiral closes, the whale's mouth appears. The strong propelling motions used as the net is blown force the body of the whale up and out of the water until frequently the entire head and mouth are exposed. If the feed is engulfed just below the water's surface, a flash of smaller bubbles is caused by the closure of the whale's mouth on the now-enlarged previously blown bubbles. The whale rights himself and takes a breath only to start the procedure over again.

The bubblenet can be executed by a single animal, or two animals can blow a doubled net, with the outside whale working a bit harder to catch up for a simultaneous finish, which finds the huge animals lying in echelon at the surface with their mouths close together. Often during this maneuver, the huge lower jaw of one whale will fall in an obviously coordinated but not too light thump upon the bridge of the companion's nose.

A number of body cuts are gained during bubblenet feeding especially when the feeding partner has a heavy encrustation of barnacles on its chin or when the pads on the forward edge of the flippers of the partner have acorn barnacles, a common variety in Alaska's inshore waters. These cuts, though numerous, are superficial, for the whale is relatively thick skinned.

On some occasions, when two whales cooperate in blowing a bubblenet to corral herring, a whale "song"

can be heard. During the blowing of the net, a low buzz similar to that of a captive bee can be heard. As the final bubbles approach the surface, the song changes to a staccato of higher-pitched sounds. A second or two later herring appear at the surface. The feeding song has been heard only in association with more than one whale feeding and only when the feed is herring.

Although feeding is a common activity of the humpback in Southeastern Alaska, as the summer progresses and feed is plentiful, the long periods of feeding are broken by the very real need to rest. The resting and sleeping methods of a humpback provide exciting and unforgettable moments for an observer. A resting humpback may, at times, move slowly at the surface with the movements of tide or current, or it may hover slightly below the water's surface at a depth of 4 to 10 feet, rising each 90 seconds for a breath, and then sinking below the surface to continue its snooze.

When a sleeping humpback lies close to the surface, it looks like a low dark rock, awash. The blowhole and dorsal fin of a sleeping adult humpback are below the water's surface, but calves, apparently still light enough in the posterior, float with the dorsal fin and blowhole above the surface. The flippers and tail hang pendulously. During surface sleeping, the blowhole is sealed with a positive pressure, attested to by a row of tiny bubbles that can be seen and heard escaping along the center flap of each of the nostrils. The nose inflates, rising a foot from its at-rest position. The nostrils pop open and a breath is explosively exhaled and then inhaled. The nostrils audibly slap closed. The nose collapses and the whale continues its slumber. The humpback has two nostrils which, when open, produce apertures about the size of two very large grapefruit. A humpback will sleep one to two hours unless disturbed, and calves rest more frequently than adults.

Although people have suggested for years that humpbacks mate and calve in Alaskan waters, there are no recorded observations of such. If the whales do migrate to warmer waters to mate and calve, they would have to travel much faster than their usual travel

A sleeping humpback calf with its blowhole just visible at the near edge of its exposed body. (Charles Jurasz)

Tracking Humpback Whales

Charts below and at right trace the movements of the whale-research vessel *Ginjur,* operated by Charles and Ginny Jurasz and family, during July 1977 cruises in Southeastern Alaskan waters. As the keys indicate, the solid red line is the path of the *Ginjur;* other colors represent the paths taken by humpback whales, cruise ships, tour boats and a sailboat. By correlating positions of whales with approaching vessels — and by simultaneously studying behavior patterns of whales as "strangers" enter the area — the Jurasz family has learned to accurately predict how whales will respond to different intruders — from cruise ships to kayaks. (Predictably, the whales are most alarmed when large cruise ships approach.) These charts were adapted from meticulous hand-written logs kept by crewmembers aboard the *Ginjur.*

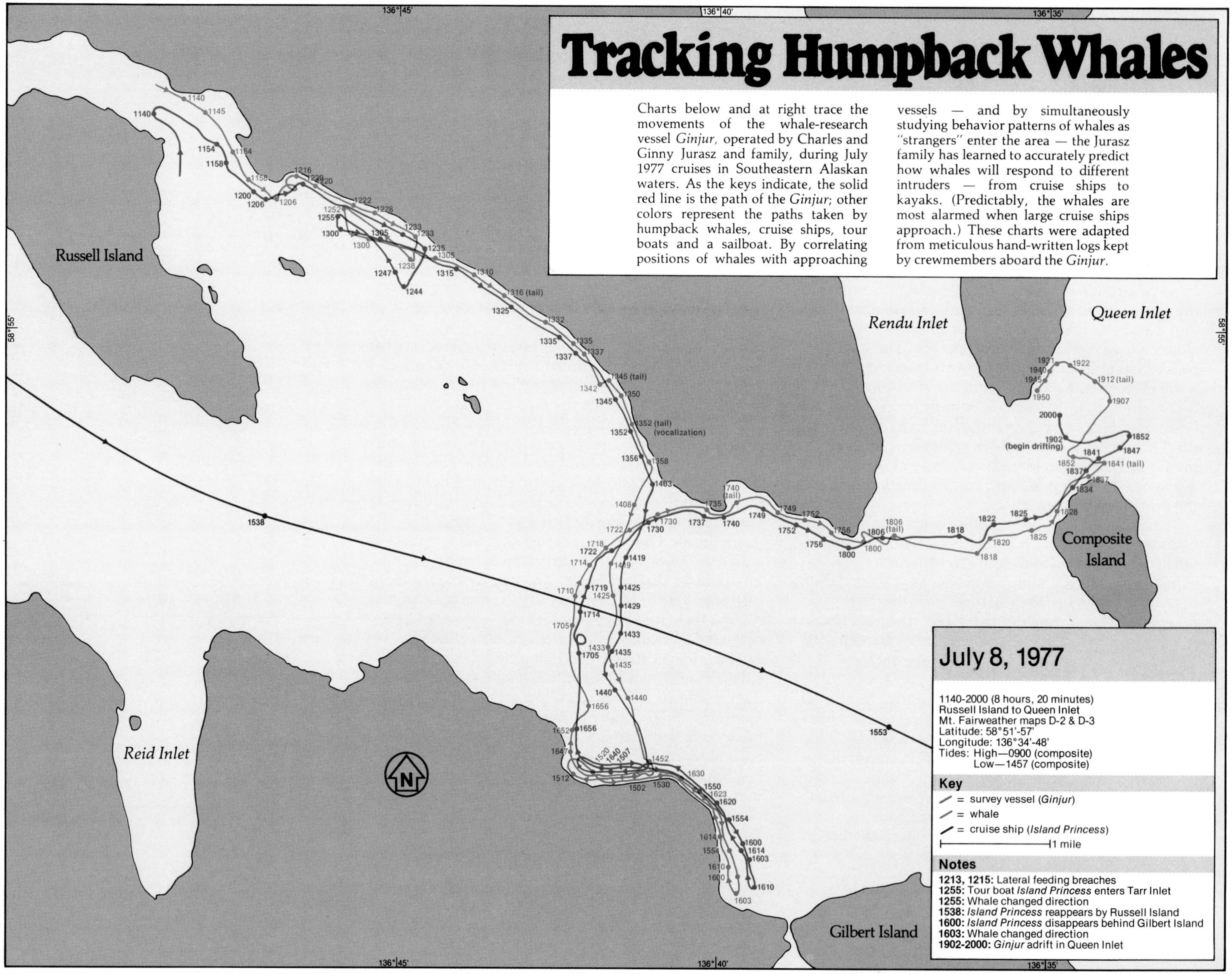

Russell Island

Reid Inlet

Rendu Inlet

Queen Inlet

Composite Island

Gilbert Island

July 8, 1977

1140-2000 (8 hours, 20 minutes)
Russell Island to Queen Inlet
Mt. Fairweather maps D-2 & D-3
Latitude: 58°51'-57'
Longitude: 136°34'-48'
Tides: High—0900 (composite)
        Low—1457 (composite)

Key

⟋ = survey vessel (*Ginjur*)
⟋ = whale
⟋ = cruise ship (*Island Princess*)
|————————| 1 mile

Notes

1213, 1215: Lateral feeding breaches
1255: Tour boat *Island Princess* enters Tarr Inlet
1255: Whale changed direction
1538: *Island Princess* reappears by Russell Island
1600: *Island Princess* disappears behind Gilbert Island
1603: Whale changed direction
1902-2000: *Ginjur* adrift in Queen Inlet

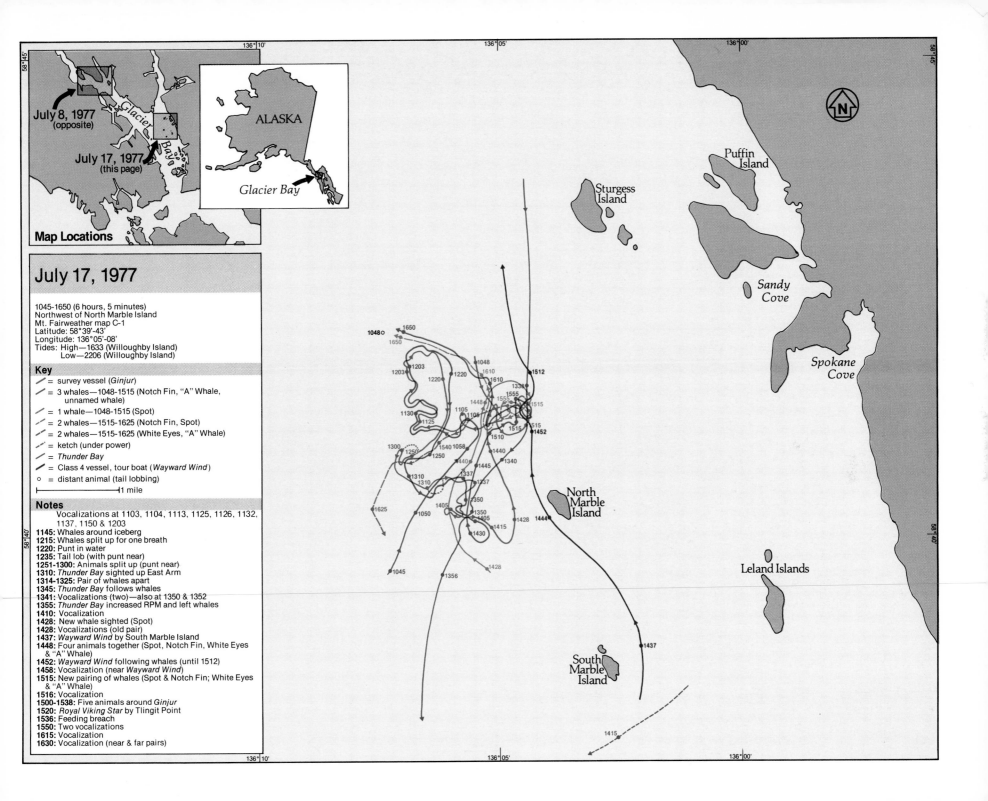

Map Locations

July 8, 1977
(opposite)

July 17, 1977
(this page)

ALASKA

Glacier Bay

July 17, 1977

1045-1650 (6 hours, 5 minutes)
Northwest of North Marble Island
Mt. Fairweather map C-1
Latitude: 58°39'-43'
Longitude: 136°05'-08'
Tides: High—1633 (Willoughby Island)
Low—2206 (Willoughby Island)

Key

⟋	= survey vessel (*Ginjur*)
⟋	= 3 whales—1048-1515 (Notch Fin, "A" Whale, unnamed whale)
⟋	= 1 whale—1048-1515 (Spot)
⟋	= 2 whales—1515-1625 (Notch Fin, Spot)
⟋	= 2 whales—1515-1625 (White Eyes, "A" Whale)
⟋	= ketch (under power)
⟋	= *Thunder Bay*
⟋	= Class 4 vessel, tour boat (*Wayward Wind*)
○	= distant animal (tail lobbing)
	⊢————⊣ 1 mile

Notes

Vocalizations at 1103, 1104, 1113, 1125, 1126, 1132, 1137, 1150 & 1203
1145: Whales around iceberg
1215: Whales split up for one breath
1220: Punt in water
1235: Tail lob (with punt near)
1251-1300: Animals split up (punt near)
1310: *Thunder Bay* sighted up East Arm
1314-1325: Pair of whales apart
1345: *Thunder Bay* follows whales
1341: Vocalizations (two)—also at 1350 & 1352
1355: *Thunder Bay* increased RPM and left whales
1410: Vocalization
1428: New whale sighted (Spot)
1428: Vocalizations (old pair)
1437: *Wayward Wind* by South Marble Island
1448: Four animals together (Spot, Notch Fin, White Eyes & "A" Whale)
1452: *Wayward Wind* following whales (until 1512)
1458: Vocalization (near *Wayward Wind*)
1515: New pairing of whales (Spot & Notch Fin; White Eyes & "A" Whale)
1516: Vocalization
1500-1538: Five animals around *Ginjur*
1520: *Royal Viking Star* by Tlingit Point
1536: Feeding breach
1550: Two vocalizations
1615: Vocalization
1630: Vocalization (near & far pairs)

The R.V. *Ginjur*, a 50-foot whale research vessel especially equipped for near-silent running, approaches a humpback. The *Ginjur* is so quiet that a man swimming alongside the idling vessel can only hear a tick similar to that of an alarm clock. (Bruce Wellman, courtesy of Charles Jurasz)

126

rate of about four knots in order to reach Southern California or Hawaii, and return in time to be seen in early April in Alaska. Perhaps only a portion of the population leaves to mate and calve, and a portion of the population remains. Another suggestion is that the Alaskan humpback mates and calves on the outer coast of Alaska. As more becomes known about the life history of the humpback and its migration routes, the questions concerning mating and calving of the Alaskan humpback will be answered.

Humpback whales appear to have a complex social order involving very specific behaviors that relate to Alaska. More than 12 years and 15,000 hours of observations of the humpback in Southeastern are beginning to disclose the patterns of the whale's natural history, patterns that include the interactions with other humpbacks, with killer whales, with vessels, with aircraft and with other phenomena which at first glance may seem unrelated. The platform from which the observations are made is the R.V. *Ginjur*, 50-foot wooden vessel equipped with a single Perkins diesel engine with a Navy exhaust silencer, which cruises at eight knots. Both the shaft and propeller are bronze with a rubber mounting coupling. Exhaust sounds and sounds transmitted through the hull have been so scrutinized and reduced that when a man is swimming alongside of the idling vessel, he can only hear a tick similar to that of an alarm clock.

The data and observations are recorded in a series of logs developed over the years and through photographic records which are used to establish identification of the whales and to aid in studying behavior.

If each facet of the humpback's life is grasped as an isolated unit, the picture of its life will lack dimension. The whale's medium is water. A whale does not always need to lie horizontal to the earth or to the water's surface, but can hang upside down or stand on its head effortlessly.

Our thinking which has long neglected all but the surface of the sea, has left us with a system of comparisons that are literally landlocked. In the ocean, the humpback grazes upon euphausiids and fish as if they were sedentary, as if they were a grass. The terrestrial equivalent would be a land animal cruising along scooping up small animals and birds, at a rate of speed comparable to that of a human jogger, but weighing in at four tons while still tagging along with its mother. That would be a bad dream, a return to prehistoric times, or a Hollywood special. Man is not often prepared to think in terms of fluid mechanics and what it allows and prevents in terms of life forms.

A whale sees that all circles are not flat and two-dimensional. The greatness of a whale is not only a measure of its immensity, but also the beauty of its motion in an underwater world, where a circle is a sphere. □

Editor's note: *Chuck Jurasz and family, including his wife Ginny and children, Susan, 15, and Peter, 10, live aboard the R.V.* Ginjur *year-around, studying whales full-time during summer months. Jurasz teaches biology and oceanography at Juneau-Douglas High School.*

Chuck Jurasz, right, and a research assistant, Peter Tyack, study a chart of Glacier Bay in the wheelhouse of the R.V. *Ginjur* during an early summer search for humpbacks. (Marty Loken, Staff)

By LAEL MORGAN

The Study of Whales

Whales in Captivity

Because of their size and man's lack of knowledge of what makes a healthy environment for whales, few of the large whale species have been maintained successfully in captivity. Only killer whales and belugas seem to have adapted well to a contained environment and individuals of these species have been performing at sea life parks for several years. Thus, when personnel at Sea World in San Diego corralled Gigi, a gray whale calf (see "Gray Whales" page 76) in Scammon's Lagoon off Baja California on March 13, 1971, it was a noteworthy event in the history of whales in captivity. During her time at Sea World Gigi gained 10,000 pounds, grew 9 feet in length, and increased her appetite from 180 pounds to 2,000 pounds of food daily which was sound reason for sending her back to the wild. Occasional reports of sightings of Gigi since her release have led scientists to believe that she survived her return to freedom.

Sea World, which is the largest operation of its type in the world, has 20 full-time trainers for marine mammals, and a sizable pod of killer and beluga whales. Bruce Stephens, director of animal behavior for the organization, admits that personnel at Sea World haven't gotten all the answers yet but that understanding of the behavior of smaller whales has come a long way in a short time.

"The killer whale is easier to train than a dog. It is the fastest learner among the cetaceans and has no natural fear. The killer whale comes right up to the trainer on the first day. I believe its spot at the very top of the ecosystem has something to do with its responsiveness. The killer whale is the top predator in the ocean . . . and

as with humans, the most confident is going to succeed," asserts Stephens.

Age is not much of a factor in training a killer whale and a subject which is not interested in training at one point may respond enthusiastically a year or two later. "Sometimes an animal simply does not adapt well to training and if that's the case, we simply let it alone . . . maybe the animal will be hot two years later," Stephens explains.

Sea World deliberately avoids assigning one animal to one trainer on a permanent basis. Instead, the organization rotates its staff so that the whales deal with several different people.

Rewards of food are used, Stephens says, but on a random basis mixed with praise, affection and rubdowns. "Food deprivation works effectively, it's easy and some outfits do use it, but I think it's morally reprehensible."

There are other incentives, though, like separating a whale from its friend and rewarding it with a visit when it masters a new trick. A new toy is another effective award. "The killer whale loves to play," asserts Stephens. "It invents games to play with other whales."

Stephens cares very much for his charges and he bristles at any aspersions cast on the disposition of the killer whale. "It's not vicious at all, if handled correctly," he insists. "In the wild the killer is a subsistence hunter which must kill to live."

Spared the necessity of the hunt, however, the killer is well behaved, Stephens reports. "I've been bitten several times—nothing serious—but if the animal wanted to, it could cut a person in half."

One of Sea World's main attractions is a show entitled "Shamu Goes to College" in which the killer

TOP — One of Sea World's captive belugas swims by for a closer look. (Lael Morgan, Staff)
ABOVE — A trained killer whale rests at poolside at Sea World. (Lael Morgan, Staff)

LEFT — Corky, a female killer whale, jumps on command at Marineland in Los Angeles. (Penny Rennick, Staff)

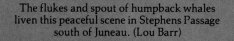

The flukes and spout of humpback whales liven this peaceful scene in Stephens Passage south of Juneau. (Lou Barr)

Whale Sounds

When scientists drew up plans to assess the bowhead population in 1978, one technique was to use a hydrophone to record whale sounds and thereby get a count of the number of animals. What is surprising is that they had no reference recordings of bowheads from which to work.

"Except for the echolocating abilities of the porpoises and a few behaviors associated with sound production, very little is known about the significance of underwater sound to marine mammals—and virtually nothing [is known] where the large whales are concerned," observes Dr. William C. Cummings, chief scientist at the Natural History Museum in San Diego.

The Navy first recorded whale sounds during World War II in order to distinguish them from the more important submarine noises which they were monitoring.

About 1970 John Vania, a biologist with the Alaska Department of Fish & Game, acquired a recording of killer whale screams and, wrapping his auto tape deck in a plastic bag, projected their sounds into the waters inland of Bristol Bay where beluga whales were swimming. Killer whales prey upon belugas and, as Vania suspected, the belugas turned tail and disappeared when they heard the sounds from the killer whale tape. Belugas, in turn, prey on salmon fry and Vania reasoned correctly that killer whale sounds played at river mouths during spawning season might keep belugas at bay and thus allow for better salmon escapement. Further development of this idea resulted in the Bendix Corporation manufacturing "Beluga Repellers" for the State of Alaska. Biologists report that the program has been effective so far, but there's a growing suspicion that the technique may have produced a new generation of careless belugas that swim out to sea, ignore sounds of actual killer whales and are eaten.

Cummings had an opportunity to observe southern right whales and was puzzled when he discovered that they were unaffected by killer whale recordings, although killer whales are definitely their enemies. Cummings and Paul O. Thompson, who also worked on the project, observed that humpback whales in Hawaii and those in Alaska have vastly different repertoires. The whales in Alaska, which spend a good deal of their time feeding, trumpet and make low-frequency pulses. The humpbacks in Hawaii, which are primarily mating and calving, sing complex songs that last from 7 to 30 minutes and are repeated for hours.

Could it be that the right whales, observed off Argentina, were not familiar with the killer whale sounds played by Cummings and Thompson because those killers had been recorded off the coast of Washington State? The same recordings of killers definitely frightened gray whales migrating in the Northern Hemisphere; perhaps, scientists reason, the vocabulary of the Southern Hemisphere killer whales is different.

In working with blue whales, Cummings and Thompson were startled to record the most powerful sounds ever heard from animals, which they estimated could be detected with a hydrophone hundreds of miles away.

Most scientists agree that the other large whales do not use sound as a navigation aid in the manner of active sonar.

"Who knows what they use for bearings. I'm sure they've got something going for them besides visual clues that we don't understand," Cummings asserts. And he subscribes to the theory that sounds are used as a means of communication among whales.

At this point, however, scientists seem to be a long way from translating whale sounds. For one thing, it's often difficult for the recording scientists to see what a whale is doing when it is being taped. And often observation is confusing. Gray whales, for example, are known as quiet whales, but they groan and mutter on migration. And scientists are puzzled over the rumble coming from apparently inactive blue whales. Perhaps

the noise is a "rhythmic bodily function" . . . a stomach growl?

Baleen whales generally have low-pitched voices whereas their toothed cousins emit higher frequency and more variable sounds, according to Cummings and Thompson.

Navy researchers suspect they inadvertently may have recorded bowheads from an isolated station near the Bering Strait on April 6, and December 29, 1977.

"At first we thought they were humpback sounds, but Dr. George Harry [Marine Mammal Division, National Marine Fisheries], points out that humpbacks don't go near that region at that time of year because of the ice . . . so it must be bowheads," Thompson reasons.

Even if bowhead recordings are clearly identified, it remains a problem to discover under just what conditions the animals vocalize. And if they migrate in silence, hydrophone will obviously not help in counting them.

It may well be that scientists will have to wait for technology to advance before they learn all they need to know about whale sounds. But fortunately, scientists are really interested in this area and funding for study is more readily available than in years past. □

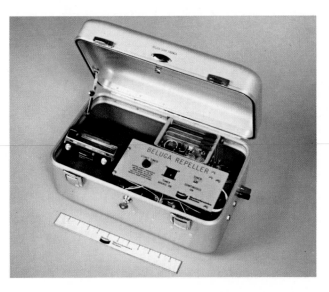

A "Beluga Repeller." The machine is set in a boat or on a pier and sounds of killer whales are projected through an underwater loudspeaker to keep belugas away from salmon. Alaska Department of Fish & Game personnel have reported a noticeable effect on beluga behavior up to 15 miles from the loudspeaker. (Courtesy of Bendix Corporation)

Eskimo whalers paddle on a glassy sea in search of bowheads.
INSET — The darting gun used in taking whales. The gun has a bomb and (in the gun on the right) a harpoon attached. The bomb is released when the trigger (the metal rod to the left of the bomb) touches the whale. (Both photos by John Bockstoce)

By LAEL MORGAN

Modern Eskimo Whaling

Before the turn of the last century Charles Dewitt Brower, a white whaler and trader in Barrow, made the innovative decision to utilize traditional Eskimo whalers in his hunt for bowheads and reported that at first they made fun of him for keeping a recently invented whaling gun in readiness.

"The men had hardly returned to their boats and were still flinging back jibes when the first whale anyone had seen in days broke directly in front of the *umiak*. There was only time to grab a handy whale-gun and shoot before it pitched to go under the ice . . ," he wrote in his autobiography, *Fifty Years Below Zero.*

"Whether or not my eleventh-hour success with a bombgun made any deep impression on the Eskimos, the spring of 1888 marked the last season in which they kept to their old whaling customs. After that the younger crowd began more generally to adopt our whaling gear, tackles, guns, bombs and all."

Ironically, the Eskimos were still using this same "modern" equipment when they were taken to task in 1977 by conservationists and subsequently by the International Whaling Commission (IWC) for killing too many whales. Some critics insisted that if the Eskimos were going to hunt for subsistence they should return to traditional ways, thus limiting their kill, while others maintained that lack of modern technology was responsible for the discouraging number of whales struck and lost.

Because skin-covered boats are most forgiving for ice navigation, most Eskimos still hunt from them as their ancestors did hundreds of years before Brower arrived. And their technique is basically the same as that of the

ABOVE — A whaler waits for his quarry off Barrow during the spring 1978 bowhead season. (Lael Morgan, Staff, reprinted from *ALASKA*® magazine)

135

Harpoon poised, Junior Slwooko of Saint Lawrence Island is ready to strike a bowhead. (Chlaus Lotscher)

ABOVE — Natives at the edge of the ice reach for a dead bowhead. Note the bladder float attached to the whale.
LEFT — Many villagers turn out to help haul the bowhead onto the ice where it can be butchered. This whale measured 52 feet and was taken by the villagers at Wainwright in the spring 1978 hunt. (Both photos by Alice Puster)

traditional period when they paddled quietly up to the mammoth whale, assailed it in a vital spot with bone or stone harpoon and encumbering float of sealskin, then bucked the whale's churning wake until the hit proved fatal or the beast tired enough to harpoon again.

Today, outboard engines are sometimes used to haul home carcasses or to reach distant whaling grounds in the fall, but the machines are too noisy for the stalk and kill, so paddles or sails (in the case of Saint Lawrence Islanders) are still the only way to go.

As it has ever been in northern Eskimo country, the most respected mark of a man is to have a whale kill to his credit. As it has always been, the whaling feast is the highlight of each year and sad is the village that cannot afford one.

What has changed in some villages is the economics of the hunt. When Eskimos lived by hunting alone there was no question but what hunters would do everything possible to bring home as much meat as they could. In recent years, however, some Native communities have

CLOCKWISE FROM RIGHT — Once the lines are attached to the whale, it takes many villagers to haul in the bowhead which can weigh many tons. / Loading whale meat onto the sleds to be taken back to the village of Wainwright. (Both photos by Alice Puster) / Lucky captain Jake Adams of Barrow divides the flipper, the choicest portion of the bowhead's meat. (Lael Morgan, Staff)

been smitten with unusual prosperity—pipeline jobs, construction booms and the like. And since whaling is as important as ever traditionally, many Eskimos who could not previously afford to outfit a boat have done so—some without the usual apprenticeship (from the age of 13 on) that makes for careful, conservative hunting.

In addition there has been a marked population increase in the Arctic. Barrow, which for centuries has lived by whaling, has grown from a few families in Brower's time to 3,300 and is now the largest Eskimo community in the United States. In 1977 there were 34 Barrow crews out on the spring hunt, almost double the number that hunted in the 1960's, which made it difficult for hunters to keep track of one another, and there were questions about the constitutionality of enforcing "self-regulation" if not all captains wished to cooperate. Social pressure once served but some villages have grown so fast that old social structures have broken down. By 1977 it became obvious it would take more than the scorn of old-timers to cut down the take and keep inept hunters off the ice.

Conservationists watched with growing alarm as the number of bowheads taken in the Arctic jumped from an annual average of 29 between 1970 and 1975 to 48 (with an additional 35 struck and lost) during the 1976 season. Some believe the bowhead is endangered and, although there were no census figures, American delegates to the IWC were told to advise the Natives that regulation of their hunt was being considered. Eskimo leaders, maintaining no such warning was delivered, were stunned when the IWC announced a total ban on whaling in mid-1977.

In negotiations later that year in Japan, Eskimo advocates managed to get a quota of 12 whales taken or 18 struck, with the establishment of the Alaska Eskimo Whaling Commission (AEWC) for self-regulation, but as a trade-off, the United States allowed the taking of an additional 5,681 sperm whales (an increase from 763 to 6,444) by commercial hunters from Japan and Russia, and left the Eskimos saddled with a penalty for quota violations—$10,000 fine and/or a year in jail.

A whale camp on the ice near Wainwright on the Chukchi Sea coast. (Lael Morgan, Staff)

As for the AEWC, "the only self-regulation involved is how the villages—9 of them—will divide up 12 whales among themselves," charged an angry Barrow youth in a public meeting.

Government officials made private assurances that if Eskimos could display self-control long enough for an accurate bowhead census, and if the population was found to be on the rise as the Eskimos and some scientists believed, the future might be brighter.

Among themselves the Eskimos decided to allow one whale each for Gambell and Savoonga (Saint Lawrence), two for Point Hope, one for Kivalina, two for Wainwright, one for Nuiqsut, one for Barter Island and three for Barrow. After quotas were set, the village of Wales (which originally did not reply to queries) asked to be included. No one could recall Wales men taking a whale in modern times, although they were traditionally expert whalers, but Thomas Napaqeak, the only captain in Nuiqsut, volunteered his whale for them, noting if Wales didn't take it during the spring

139

ABOVE — Large sections of bowhead meat dot the ice as the villagers of Wainwright prepare to haul the whale farther out of the water. (Alice Puster)
RIGHT — Cooking muktuk on gas stoves at Wainwright. Muktuk is the blubber, or fatty tissue, which separates a whale's skin from its underlying muscle. (Lael Morgan, Staff)

hunt he'd have a chance later because his whaling season is in the fall.

"It wasn't an easy thing to do but I had to do it," he said in the spirit of the day.

Hopes rose in Eskimo communities when the manufacturer of the standard whaling gun was dispatched north (at government expense) to discuss improved whaling techniques, but he talked of only a minor modification—at least a year off—on an old brass model that's been around for nearly 100 years (replacement cost roughly $900) instead of the sure-fire bomb the hunters had hoped for.

All went well at first. Savoonga and Gambell caught their quota of two whales and hauled their boats home. Point Hope, Kivalina and Wainwright were kept from the hunt by thick fog and poor ice conditions. Then the ice was clear at Barrow, conditions ideal; three whales were quickly taken and the trouble began.

In a published statement before the hunt, Borough Mayor Eben Hopson had stated, "Hopefully we will not violate the quota for the bowhead whales. There are other whales we can catch that are not called bowheads. We may catch more than three bowhead whales but if we do, it will be some other whale besides bowhead."

The Eskimos have long claimed there are two species that migrate north in spring: bowheads and a smaller type called *inutuq* which are fatter, with a decidedly different way of breaching than the bowhead. Scientists have not recognized these distinctions. Now Eskimos reported they had taken two *inutuqs* and one bowhead.

"Two more bowhead whales to go," some said.

"Another whale of any kind would be a violation," insisted federal enforcement people, as did Arnold Brower, president of the local whaling organization who feared his people would be saddled with heavy fines and a bad name.

Heated debate ensued on village CB radios. Crews came home. Crews went back on the ice. A fourth whale was taken. More argument; more anguish. Real anguish. Families were divided and frightened. A call came from Washington, D.C., to several Native leaders. No one would say who it was from but word was that valuable whaling gear would be confiscated, the $10,000 fine would be applied . . . and Barrow whale boats came off the ice. All but one.

It was Billy Neakok's first year as a captain; he'd just received the command from his father, Nate, a respected hunter and—indeed—Billy himself had always spoken for the conservative, traditional way. Neakok's mother, Sadie, had long been a Barrow magistrate. Billy was recognized as a Native leader of growing importance.

But Neakok had gone to Japan and watched U.S. delegates to the IWC give nearly 6,000 sperm whales to the Japanese and Russians to gain 12 bowheads for the Eskimos. Like many non-Natives he felt the Eskimos had become a pawn in a larger political game.

Neakok made no statement to the press. He walked out of the local whaling captains' meeting alone, against the advice of his elders, saying he wasn't going to quit until he caught a whale.

The Eskimo whaling commission had set out to demonstrate that its members could wisely manage subsistence hunting and many feared Neakok's defiance of the quota (before the census was taken) would jeopardize their chance of self-determination.

In an effort to tighten their hunting rules, the Eskimos made it unlawful to shoot a whale with a shoulder gun if there was no way to attach a float to the animal; prohibited the sharing of meat with a hunter who wouldn't help butcher, and set a fine of $1,000 for members who violated conservation standards.

Results were impressive, in the end. The total number of whales taken remained low—and, importantly, the struck-and-lost ratio dropped dramatically. Dr. Richard Frank, director of the National Oceanic and Atmospheric Administration, who visited Barrow in midseason, complimented AEWC on its work and promised if no more quotas were violated there was a good chance of getting more realistic ground rules.

As for the one Barrow violation, "The fourth whale seems to me to be an honest dispute and we have now

TOP — Whaling is done primarily from skin boats that are lightweight, fast and easy to maneuver in the ice. Here the Leavitt brothers of Barrow stretch the hide of a bearded seal which will cover the wooden frame of a skin boat, or *umiak*.
ABOVE — To make the cover watertight the sealskin is joined together with a special seam sewn with sinew. (Both photos by Rob Stapleton, Anchorage Daily News)

Sunset at a Barrow whaling camp. Mukluks, or fur boots, hang on the tent posts at right, within easy reach in case a bowhead should pass by. (Alice Puster)

clarified it and prosecution would now be inappropriate," Dr. Frank said.

Whalers pressed Frank to reveal what would happen if there were future violations but he refused to commit himself, saying only that "this community will suffer for it and I will suffer for it," alluding to his efforts to increase the Eskimo quota in the face of IWC protest.

The Department of the Interior went on record, at the height of the Barrow controversy, saying no Eskimo family would go hungry as a result of the limited bowhead take—an assurance no man had had when he pulled in his boat.

Greenpeace, which had supported a total moratorium on the killing of bowheads, sent two observers who camped with hunters and reported "insight into how difficult it is for these people to actually find, strike and kill a bowhead whale."

Elizabeth Tillbury, a member of the team, said "from what we have observed it appears that the people in Barrow use all parts of the whale and it is an integral part of their diet," and added Greenpeace might show some sympathy with Eskimos in the future.

The Alaska Center for the Environment noted a "strong recognition within the state that the rapid advancement of technology and increasing economic demands pose a threat to both the great sea mammals and the people that depend on them. Both should and can be saved."

And Monitor, an alliance of 27 conservation agencies including the Sierra Club, Humane Society and Rare Animal Relief Effort, went on record as "supporting a limited subsistence take based on traditional needs if it is scientifically acceptable that the species is not endangered."

Meanwhile, with a last-minute infusion of money, the National Marine Fisheries Service more than doubled its bowhead research effort. The 1978 season resulted in an accumulation of new facts on the great whale, and release—not long after the whaling effort ended—of an official population guesstimate that there are 2,264 bowheads in the world.

In light of this news (earlier estimates placed the bowhead population at 1,000 to 2,000), the Eskimos asked for a 1979 quota of 37 whales, and were partially supported by the U.S. delegation to the IWC, which urged an increase from 12 to 24 animals.

The commission wouldn't go that far, however. The 1979 quota was set at 18, over the protests of the Alaska Eskimo Whaling Commission and others.

What's the future of subsistence whaling?

142

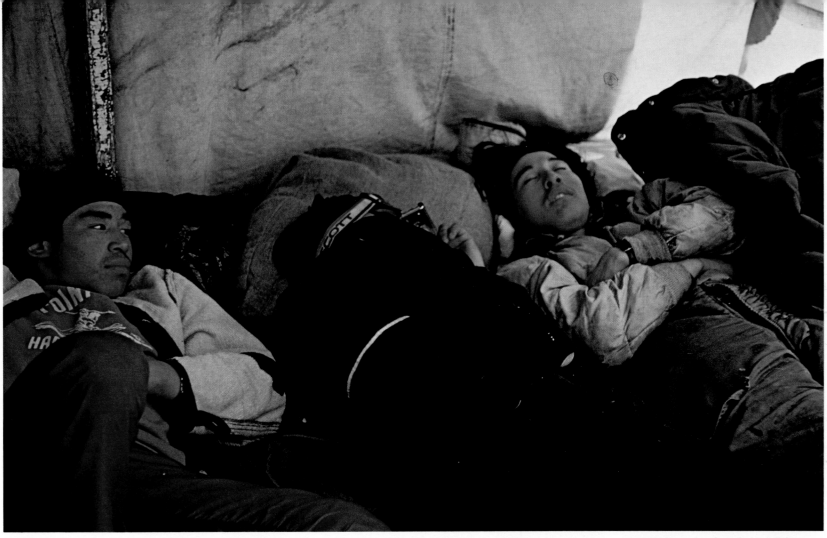

Certainly, the Eskimos have seen their last 48-whale season . . . never again will uncontrolled subsistence whaling be allowed. Tighter controls and changing lifestyles may eventually wipe out the traditional—and nutritional demand—that Eskimos hunt bowhead whales.

But even the end of hunting will not guarantee the return of great numbers of bowheads, for they also are threatened by industry in the Arctic.

"The bowhead whale," concludes William Aron, United States commissioner to the IWC, "is the most fragile of all whale populations in the world today, not only because of whaling, but also because of North Slope oil-related activities—and I'm not just talking about oil spills.

"Human presence in any area where there are bowhead whales disrupts their breeding . . . and threatens the entire population."□

Whaling is hard work. Here Eskimos grab what rest they can at a whale camp near Wainwright. (Lael Morgan, Staff)

FOLLOWING PAGE— Spray from one humpback whale fills the air as a companion begins to dive in Glacier Bay. (William Boehm)

143